EDWARD BIBBINS AVELING

THE STUDENTS' MARX

AN INTRODUCTION TO THE STUDY OF

KARL MARX' CAPITAL

Elibron Classics
www.elibron.com

Elibron Classics series.

ISBN 1-4021-9925-2 (paperback)
ISBN 1-4021-1439-7 (hardcover)

This Elibron Classics Replica Edition is an unabridged facsimile of the edition published in 1902 by Swan Sonnenschein & Co., Ltd., London.

THE STUDENTS' MARX

An Introduction to the Study of

KARL MARX' *CAPITAL.*

BY

EDWARD AVELING

D.Sc., London; Fellow of University College, London

LONDON

SWAN SONNENSCHEIN & CO., LIM.

PATERNOSTER SQUARE

NEW YORK: CHARLES SCRIBNERS' SONS

1902

INTRODUCTION.

THE present work is an attempt to do for part of the writings of Karl Marx that which, in the "Students Darwin," I tried to do for the whole of the writings of Charles Darwin. The "Students' Marx" is intended for those who have read, and for those who have not read, the English translation of the first volume of "Das Kapital" that has been published by Messrs. Sonnenschein. To both, this volume may be of use as a brief analysis of the main facts, reasonings, and conclusions to be found in so much of "Das Kapital" as is at present rendered into English.

Although there is a second volume of the work out in Germany, and although the third volume is nearly ready for publication in that country, and although, as yet, neither of these has been translated into English, the first volume, of which an analysis is here attempted, is complete in itself.

Perhaps, at some future time, it may be possible to make the "Students' Marx" complete, not only by incorporating with it an account of the two other parts of "Das Kapital," but also by incorporating with it an account of the other writings of Marx. In the meantime, this analysis is, I hope, like the work of which it is an epitome, complete in itself.

Between Darwin and Marx there is resemblance in many ways. They were contemporary. Darwin was born in 1809 and died in 1882. Marx was born in 1818 and died in 1883. The physical presence of each was commanding. It is difficult—perhaps it is impossible—to find in the pictures of the nineteenth-century men and women two heads of such singular strength and beauty as those of Darwin and Marx. In moral character the two men were alike. The most bitter of their enemies—and they both had many very bitter enemies—have had to confess, if only by silence, to the truthfulness, rectitude, and purity of life characteristic of both men. The nature of each was beautiful, kindling affection in, and giving affection to, all that was worthy. They were, of necessity, subject during life to the grossest calumny and misrepresentation, and they both lived down and outlived all this.

To the student, not unmindful of this physical and moral parallel, the mental similarity between the two men is perhaps of most moment. That which Darwin did for Biology, Marx has done for Economics. Each of them by long and patient observation, experiment, recordal, reflection, arrived at an immense generalisation,—a generalisation the like of which their particular branch of science had never seen; a generalisation that not only revolutionised that branch, but is actually revolutionising the whole of human thought, the whole of human life. And that the generalisation of Darwin is at present much more universally accepted than that of Marx is probably due to the fact that the former affects our intellectual rather than our economic life—can, in a word, be accepted in a measure alike by the believers in the capitalistic system and by its opponents. There can be little doubt that the two names by which the nineteenth century will be known, as far as its thinking is concerned, will be those of Charles Darwin and Karl Marx.

One difference between the two may be noted. Marx was the more universal. Darwin was, confessedly, a man given up to biological, or, at most, to scientific work, in the restricted sense of the term. Marx was, on the other hand, master, in the fullest sense, not only of his special subject, but of all branches of science, of seven or eight different languages, of the literature of Europe. He knew and loved all forms of art—poetry and the drama most of all.

Another difference between the two men—with the advantage on the side of the economic philosopher

—is that he was not only a philosopher, but a man of action. Marx was an active leader of men and of organisations. Thousands of workers, of both sexes and all lands, who may never read a line of his philosophical writings, know him and love him as the practical revolutionist, who, more than any other, helped to make the great working-class revolt of the nineteenth century, and as long as he lived took an active and informing part in it.

And Marx had that with which no one can conscientiously credit Darwin, a huge sense of humour, and a singularly brilliant style, even in dealing with abstruse problems. Obviously, nothing of these two qualities can be shown in this work. For them the reader must turn to the writings of Marx himself.

I propose in this volume to make use of the plan of key-notes found so useful in the writing of books for, and in the teaching of, scientific students. The words and phrases at the side of the pages will be of use to the reader as key-notes to the subject-matter. A good test of the mastery of this by the student is the taking these side-notes in succession, or at random, and observing if the facts and principles given in connexion with them in the text can be substantially reproduced from memory.

The mathematical form in which Marx puts many of his generalisations will be retained. The reasons, the necessity for doing this are obvious. (1) Marx himself used this form. (2) It is, even to the student with little or no knowledge of mathematics, a convenient and easily understandable method of noting certain facts and generalisations in the briefest and the plainest way. (3) A science has only reached a stable condition when its truths can be expressed in mathematical terms. Electricity has now its ohms, its farads, its ampères; chemistry has its periodic law; the physiologists are reducing the bodily functions to equations; and the fact that Marx could express many of his generalisations in Political Economy in mathematical terms is so much evidence that he had carried that science further than his predecessors.

The law of Hegel, referred to on p. 70 and elsewhere, is, that quantitative alteration involves qualitative change. A good illustration of this law is afforded by the innumerable series of carbon compounds (the alcohols, *e.g.*), the members of which only differ in quantitative composition by multiples of C H^2 (one atom of carbon and two atoms of hydrogen), but have very different properties.

CONTENTS.

PART I.—COMMODITIES AND MONEY.

PART II.—THE TRANSFORMATION OF MONEY (*M*) INTO CAPITAL (*C*).

PART III.—THE PRODUCTION OF ABSOLUTE SURPLUS-VALUE.

PART IV.—PRODUCTION OF RELATIVE SURPLUS-VALUE.

PART VIII.—THE SO-CALLED PRIMITIVE ACCUMULATION.

THE STUDENTS' MARX.

—:-O-:—

BOOK I.

CAPITALIST PRODUCTION

(*The only subject to be considered in this work*).

PART I.—COMMODITIES AND MONEY.

CHAPTER I.—COMMODITIES.

SECTION 1.—THE THREE VALUES.

Wealth.—Wealth is an accumulation of commodities or wares. The unit in political economy is therefore the commodity.

Commodity.—A commodity (1) is an external object; (2) satisfies human wants; (3) has human labour embodied in it; (4) is not consumed by the producer, but by some other person.

Quality and Quantity.—A commodity may be considered from the two points of view of quality and

A

quantity. This antithesis between quality and quantity is very frequent in Marx, and runs through the whole of his investigation.

Use-Value.—From the point of view of quality we are led to the consideration of the utility or use-value of a commodity. Use-values are intrinsic to, and cannot exist apart from, commodities; they form the basis of commerce, the substance of wealth, are realised when commodities are consumed, and are the material depositaries of the third kind of value,—exchange-value.

Value.—From the point of view of quantity we are led to the consideration of the exchange-value of a commodity, and we are led to it by way of the value of the commodity, as distinct from its use-value. Leaving out of consideration the utilities of commodities, they have all one common property. They are all the product of human labour, not of any particular kind of human labour, but of human labour in the abstract. The value of a commodity is the amount of abstract human labour embodied in it.

Its Measure.—And that amount is measured by the average social time required to produce the commodity under average conditions and with average ability on the part of the labourer.

V and Q.—The value of a commodity depends upon, or, in mathematical language, varies with the quantity of human labour embodied in it. If its value is represented by V, and the quantity of human labour embodied in it is represented by Q, then V varies directly as Q. The greater Q is, the greater V is; the less Q is, the less V is. The sign for "varies as" is $\propto$, so that we can write in short the statement that the value of a commodity varies directly as the quantity of human labour embodied in it, thus—$V \propto Q$.

V and P.—V, as we have seen, represents the value of a commodity, *i.e.* the amount of abstract human labour embodied in it. Let P represent the productiveness of labour. The less P is, the greater is the labour-time necessary for the production of the commodity, and therefore the greater is V. And the greater P is, the less is the labour-time necessary for the production of the commodity, and therefore the less is V. So that V varies not directly as P, but inversely as P. This is expressed in mathematical language thus—$V \propto \frac{1}{P}$.

$V \propto \frac{Q}{P}$.—Combining these two statements, that $V \propto Q$, and $V \propto \frac{1}{P}$, we have $V \propto \frac{Q}{P}$; *i.e.* the value of a commodity varies as the quantity of human labour embodied in it, and inversely as the productiveness of that labour, as determined by the state of scientific knowledge, the social and physical conditions, etc.

Exchange-Value.—The ratio in which use-values exchange. The form of expression of the value, as distinct from use-value, of a commodity.

Illustrations.—A diamond, *e.g.*, is rare. Its discovery costs, upon an average, much labour-time. Hence its value, and therefore its exchange-value, are great. Air is an example of a use-value that has, normally, no value, and therefore no exchange-value. When, by human labour, it is pumped into a diving-bell, it has all the three values. An article produced for the personal consumption of the producer is a use-value but not a commodity.

SECTION 2.—THE TWOFOLD CHARACTER OF THE LABOUR EMBODIED IN COMMODITIES.

Concrete and Abstract.—Marx claims that he has been the first to point out and examine critically the twofold nature of the labour embodied in a commodity. Once more, we have to consider the qualitative and the quantitative aspect—of labour this time, not of the commodity produced by labour. Useful, concrete, productive labour, as that of a tailor or a spinner working upon matter, *e.g.* cotton, counts qualitatively in the use-value of the product, *e.g.* yarn. Abstract human labour, the labour of the worker, not as tailor or spinner, but as labourer, counts quantitatively in the value of the commodity. Use-values are combinations of matter and concrete labour. Values represent human labour in the abstract.

Work and Labour.—The concrete labour which creates use-values and counts qualitatively is work; the abstract labour which creates value and counts quantitatively is labour. Skilled labour counts only as a multiple of unskilled labour. Henceforth, therefore, throughout the work every kind of labour is regarded as reduced to simple, unskilled labour. As yet, there is no question of wages or the value that a labourer receives. It is, at present, only a question of the value the labourer himself has put into the commodity produced.

Summary.—The rest of this very important and difficult section is devoted to the repeated presentation of the principles noted above, and ends, as so many of Marx' sections and chapters end, with an invaluable summing-up paragraph. "On the one hand all labour is, speaking physiologically, an expenditure of human labour-power, and in its character of identical abstract human labour, it creates and forms the value of commodities. On the other hand, all labour is the expenditure of human labour-power in a special form and with a definite aim, and in this, its character of concrete, useful labour, it produces use-values."

SECTION 3.—THE FORM OF VALUE OR EXCHANGE-VALUE.

Social Reality.—Value is not a material, but a social, reality; and commodities only acquire this social reality in so far as they are embodiments of a social substance,—human labour. Value, therefore, can only manifest itself in the social relation between commodities.

A. *Elementary Form of Value.*

$xA = yB$.—The simplest value-relation is that of one commodity to some other commodity. $xA = yB$. Here x and y stand for any numbers, 1, 10, 25, 43, etc., and A and B for any two different commodities, as linen and coat, coat and linen, iron and wheat, etc.

1. The two poles of this elementary form.

Poles.—The value of the commodity A is expressed in terms of the other commodity B. A functions as the relative form of value, B as the equivalent form of value. These two forms are polar, and, like the North and South poles of a magnet, are mutually dependent and inseparable, but are also mutually exclusive and face to face.

Having marked off these two forms, the relative and the equivalent, each of them is now to be considered.

2. Relative form.

(*a*) Nature and import.

Qualitative Unit.—The equation xA = yB must be considered at first solely from the qualitative side, not as vulgar economy always considers it, wholly and solely from the quantitative side. A quantitative equation implies some qualitative unit. That unit is abstract human labour. The value of the commodity A, *e.g.* linen, is expressed by the actual material bodily form of the commodity B, *e.g.* a coat. The value of A is expressed by the use-value of B.

Labour-Power and Labour.—In this section we, for the first time, meet with the distinction between labour-power and labour. Labour is labour-power in action. There may be labour-power, and yet unless it is in action there is no labour, and therefore no creation of value.

(*b*) Quantitative determination of relative-value.

$V \propto \frac{1}{P}$ again.—The value form not only expresses value generally, but a definite quantity of value. But the labour-time necessary for the production of a commodity, and therefore the amount of abstract human labour embodied in the commodity, and therefore the value of the commodity vary inversely as the productiveness of labour. $V \propto \frac{1}{P}$ (see p. 3). Marx then takes four cases in which such variations affect the quantitative aspect of relative-value.

Cases.—I. When the magnitude of value of A varies,

and that of B remains constant, then the relative-value of A (its value expressed in terms of B) varies directly as the actual value of A.

II. When the magnitude of the value of B varies, and that of A remains constant, then the relative-value of A varies inversely as the actual value of B.

III. When the magnitudes of value of both A and B vary simultaneously, and in exactly the same direction and to the same extent, then their relative-values are unchanged, and their change of value can only be determined by comparison with C, a commodity whose value has not altered.

IV. When the magnitudes of value of both A and B vary simultaneously but not equally, then the results are easily deducible from I., II., III.

Conclusion.—Hence follows the important conclusion that real changes in the magnitude of value of a commodity are not *necessarily* represented in the equations expressing the magnitude of the *relative-value.* Of this incongruity between the magnitude of value and its relative expression, much use has been made by the vulgar economists.

3. The equivalent form.

Three Points.—In considering yB of the simple expression, xA=yB, three points strike us. (1) Use-value (that of B) becomes the phenomenal form (the form of manifestation) of its opposite-value (that of A). An illustration is here used to make this point more clear. A lump of sugar is balanced by a mass of iron. The iron represents only weight,—nothing else for the time being; and in the equation xA=yB, B represents only value,—nothing else for the time being. The analogy, we are warned, must not be strained too far. Weight is a natural quality; value is a social quality. (2) Concrete labour (embodied in B) becomes the phenomenal form of its opposite—abstract human labour (embodied in A). (3) The labour of an individual (that of the man who made B) becomes the phenomenal form of its opposite—social labour (that of the man who made A).

Aristotle.—Aristotle was the first to see in the expression of the value of a commodity a relation of equality. His time was, of course, long antecedent to that time in which the expression xA=yB is possible; *i.e.* long antecedent to that time in which society is a commodity-producing society.

4. The elementary form of value considered as a whole.

Summary.—This section is a summing-up of the preceding sections. A commodity contains use-value and value, even if it stands alone. Its exchange-value can only appear when it is brought into relation with some other commodity. Exchange-value is therefore a consequence, not, as the vulgar economists hold, a cause, of value. A's bodily form in the equation xA=yB only figures as use-value; B's bodily form in the equation xA = yB only figures as the form of value; so that the internal opposition within any commodity of use-value and value is, in the equation xA = yB, represented by an external opposition—that of A and B. And in this, A, whose value is to be expressed, only appears as use-value; whilst B, in terms of which the value of A is to be expressed, only appears as exchange-value.

Transition.—This simple form of the equation xA = yB only places A in relation with B. But B may be varied infinitely, and that leads to the next stage—the expanded form of value.

B. *Expanded Form of Value.*

xA = yB = zC = etc. 20 yards of linen = 1 coat = 10 lbs. of tea = etc.

1. The expanded relative form of value.

xA = yB = zC = etc.—The value of any one commodity (A), *e.g.* linen, is now expressed in terms of numberless other commodities, B, C, etc. Thus, for the first time, the value of any one commodity (A) is seen to be a congelation, not of any particular kind of human labour, but of undifferentiated human labour. And the endless series of value-equations show that it is a matter of indifference under what special form of use-value the value of the one commodity appears. For this value remains unaltered in magnitude, whether it is expressed in B or C or any other commodity. From this it is evident that it is not the exchange of commodities that regulates the magnitude of their value, but it is the magnitude of their value that regulates the proportions in which they exchange.

2. The particular equivalent form.

B, C, etc.—Considering B, C, D, etc., we see that the manifold concrete useful kinds of labour embodied in these are so many different forms of realisation of undifferentiated human labour.

3. Defects of this form.

Defects.—(*a*) It is incomplete, because the series is endless. (*b*) It consists of many independent expressions of the value of A. (*c*) Not only A's value, but the values of all other commodities have to be expressed in this way, so that we shall have an endless series of an endless series.

Transition.—But if we consider the converse relation and reverse the series, we arrive at

C. *The General Form of Value.*

$$\left.\begin{array}{r} yB \\ zC \\ etc. \end{array}\right\} \text{each} = xA.$$

1. The altered character of the form of value.

The Change.—Now all commodities express their value (*a*) in an elementary form, for they express it in one commodity, A; (*b*) with unity, for they express it in one commodity only. The use of the elementary form, $xA = yB$, and of the expanded form, $xA = yB = zC = $ etc., was to express the value of a commodity as something distinct from its use-value.

Occurrence of the Three Forms.—(1) The elementary form, $xA = yB$, occurs when the products of labour are accidentally and occasionally turned into commodities. (2) The expanded form, $xA = yB = zC = $ etc., occurs when a particular product of labour, *e.g.* cattle, is habitually exchanged for other commodities. This form distinguishes more clearly value from use-value; but as the value of A is equated with everything else, any general expression of value common to all is excluded. (3) The general form,

$$\left.\begin{array}{r} yB \\ zC \\ \text{etc.} \end{array}\right\} \text{each} = xA,$$

leads us towards money. The values of all commodities are expressed in terms of one commodity, and for the first time commodities appear as exchange-values.

Universal Equivalent.—This single commodity A is the universal equivalent, and this general value form is the reduction of all kinds of concrete labour to their common character of undifferentiated human labour.

2. Interdependent development of the relative and of the equivalent form.

Development of the Polar Antagonism.—The polar antagonism between these two forms develops as the value-form develops. In $xA = yB$, the antagonism is there, but is fluid. The equation may be reversed to $yB = xA$. In $xA = yB = zC = \text{etc.}$, only one commodity at a time can completely expand its relative-value, and the equation cannot be reversed without passing over into the general form. In

$$\left.\begin{array}{r} yB \\ zC \\ \text{etc.} \end{array}\right\} \text{each} = xA,$$

there is given to all commodities a general social relative form of value, and the antagonism between the character of A, with its direct and universal exchangeability, and the character of all other commodities, with their absence of universal exchangeability, is a polar antagonism.

3. Transition from the general form to the money form.

Money.—The universal equivalent might be any commodity. Whenever any particular commodity is socially recognised as the universal equivalent, that commodity is money. This social monopoly has been ultimately attained by gold.

D. *Money Form.*

$$\left.\begin{array}{r} yB \\ zC \\ \text{etc.} \end{array}\right\} \text{each} = x \text{ gold.}$$

Gold.—Gold is now money, because it was previously a simple commodity. It was capable of appearing upon either side of the elementary form of value, or upon either side of the expanded form of value, or upon either side of the general form of value. But now it can only appear upon the equivalent form side in equation D.

Price Form.—The expression of the relative-value of any one commodity, *e.g.* linen, in terms of money, is the price form of that commodity.

SECTION 4.—THE FETISHISM OF COMMODITIES.

Difficulty.—The difficulty in understanding a commodity does not turn upon its use-value, nor upon the factors that determine its value, *i.e.* the physiological or quantitative aspect of the labour necessary to the production of the commodity. The difficulty lies in the facts that (1) the social character of men's labour appears to be an objective character actually stamped upon the commodities that are the products of this labour, and (2) that the relation between the producers and the sum total of human labour appears not even as a relation between men, but as a relation between things,—the commodities produced.

Fetishism.—For an analogy to this definite social relation between men and the fantastic form in which it appears to them as a relation between things, we must turn to religion. Hence the use of the phrase, "Fetishism of commodities."

The Character of Labour.—The producers of commodities do not meet until they are going to exchange. Therefore the social character of their labour does not reveal itself until then.

The division of a commodity into a use-value and a value becomes of practical importance when commodities are produced for the express purpose of being exchanged. From that time, the labour of the individual has a twofold character. (1) It must satisfy a social want. (2) It must rank as an equality with the labour of others. And this twofold character of labour appears in the commodity in the facts that (1) the product must be useful to others; (2) all commodities have the common quality of value.

Producers and Commodities.—To the producers their own social action appears as the action of commodities. Commodities seem to rule producers, not to be ruled by them. But, in the midst of all the changing relations of exchange between commodities, the labour-time socially necessary for their production asserts itself as the thing that determines the value of commodities.

Conditions of Society.—Four different conditions of society are then considered. That of Robinson Crusoe; of the middle ages; of the patriarchal family; of a free community having the means of production in common.

Crusoe.—His labour, whatever form it takes, is the activity of one and the same independent Robinson, and is only a particular mode of human labour.

Middle Ages.—Here we meet with personal dependence, with services and payment in kind. The social relations between labourers appear as personal relations, and not as they do to-day, disguised under the form of social relations between commodities.

Patriarchal Family.—In the patriarchal family the products of the labour of its members are, as far as concerns the family as a whole, not commodities.

Free Community with Means of Production in Common.—The conditions are the same as those of Robinson Crusoe. All the characteristics of Crusoe's labour are here repeated, only they are social and no longer individual characteristics. The plan of work is, as with Crusoe, concerted. The products are, as with Crusoe, the property of the producers. The total product is, as with Crusoe, divided into two parts: one to be used as fresh means of social production, the other as means of subsistence for individuals.

The Individual.—The latter part is divided among the individuals according to the condition of historical and productive development attained by the community. If, *e.g.*, the individual share of the means of subsistence portion is determined by the labour-time the individual has spent, this labour-time will play a twofold part. (1) Its apportionment upon a definite social plan keeps up the proper proportion between the wants of the community and the different kinds of work to be done. (2) It serves as a measure (*a*) of the portion of the common labour to be borne by each individual; (*b*) of the share of each individual in the part of the total product told off as means of subsistence.

Religion.—The religious world is always a reflex of the social world. Thus, nowadays, individual private labour is reduced to the standard of abstract human labour; and under Christianity, abstract man is worshipped. In ancient Asiatic and other ancient modes of production, the production of commodities plays a subordinate part, the social relations between man and man are narrow, and we have in religion the worship of Nature. Religion will only finally vanish when the practical relations of life become intelligible and reasonable relations between man and man and between man and Nature

Errors of the Economists.—The rest of this chapter is devoted to the pointing out of some of the errors of the ordinary economists. (1) Their analysis of value and of the magnitude of value has been incomplete. (2) They do not distinguish between labour as it appears in the value, and labour as it appears in the use-value of a product. (3) They assume the value of one commodity (labour-power) in order to determine the values of other commodities. (4) They have not asked, still less have they answered, the question—why labour is represented by the value of its product, and labour-time is represented by the magnitude of that value. (5) They have not discovered the form under which value becomes exchange-value. (6) They assume, in many cases, that Nature plays a part in the formation of exchange-value, whereas exchange-value is only a definite social expression of the amount of labour that has been bestowed upon a commodity, and therefore Nature has nothing to do with it. (7) Gold, when functioning as money, was, under the monetary system, regarded as a natural object with strange social properties, not as the representative of a social relation between producers. The economists of to-day, looking down upon this money superstition with disdain, have themselves a similar superstition in respect to capital. (8) Some even hold that the use-value of a commodity belongs to it, independently of its material properties, while its value is part and parcel of it as a material object. This confusion has been led up to by the fact that use-values are realised without exchange, by consumption, *i.e.* by a direct relation between man and the commodity; while value is realised by exchange, *i.e.* by a social process, a relation between man and man, and between commodity and commodity. (9) Lastly, they have not understood the immense truth which Marx was the first to formulate, that the economic structure of society, *i.e.* the method of production and distribution of the products of labour, is, and always has been, the basis upon which everything else rests,—the juridical, the political, the religious, the social life of the people, no matter in what age or in what country.

CHAPTER II.—EXCHANGE.

A Social Transaction.—The juridical relation between the two persons exchanging is the reflex of the real economical relation between them. To each man his own commodity has no use-value; it is only a depositary of exchange-value. But to each man the commodity of the other has use-value and is not a depositary of exchange-value. He wants to part with his commodity in exchange for one whose use-value satisfies some want of his, and in so far the transaction is a private one. But he also desires to realise the value of his own commodity, and in so far the transaction of exchange is a social transaction.

Evolution of Exchange.—The historical evolution of exchange works out more and more fully the contrast intrinsic to all commodities between use-value and value. At the same time with this working out, and with the more and more complete conversion of products into commodities, occurs the conversion of one special commodity into money.

Stages (for the Individuals).—The stages are: (1) The production of an object that is not required to satisfy the wants of the producer, and which, therefore, has to him no use-value. (2) The transfer of this product by him to another. (3) The recognition by each of the two men concerned in the exchange that the other is a private owner of his commodity.

Stages (in Communities).—In the primitive societies that are based upon property in common, this exchange must begin upon the boundaries of the community. Thence it spreads inwards. The process is repeated and repeated. Certain products begin to be produced with a special view to exchange. Use-value begins to be distinguished from exchange-value. The quantitative proportions in which commodities exchange become fixed. The necessity of a value form grows and grows. A general social equivalent is sought for. It is now one commodity, now another. But at last one is determined upon, and that one is money.

Precious Metals.—As exchange expands, a universal general equivalent must be found. The precious metals are found to be the best commodity to fulfil the only function of money as yet considered, *i.e.* to serve as the manifestation form of the value of commodities. The precious metals have uniform qualities, and admit of much subdivision.

Use-Values of Money.—The money commodity has therefore two use-values; its special use-value as a commodity (*e.g.* gold may be used in making watches), and its formal use-value as the universal equivalent.

Money Not a Symbol.—The money form is only a

reflex in one commodity of the value relations of all commodities. The fact that money can, in certain other relations, yet to be considered, be replaced by symbols of itself (notes, cheques, etc.), leads to the mistaken idea that money is itself a symbol. It is a commodity like the rest, and its value is determined by the labour-time necessary for its production, and is expressed by the quantity of any other commodity that costs the same amount of labour-time. And this quantitative determination is made where the money commodity is produced, when it is bartered against other commodities.

The True and the False.—Gold has become money in consequence of all other commodities expressing their value in gold. The false appearance of things is that all other commodities express their value in gold, because gold is money.

CHAPTER III.—MONEY, OR THE CIRCULATION OF COMMODITIES.

SECTION 1.—THE MEASURE OF VALUES.

Function 1.—The first function of money is to be a universal measure of value. Money does not render commodities commensurable. As materialised labour, they are commensurable, and therefore their value can be thus measured.

Price.—The expression of the value of a commodity in terms of gold is its price. Price is the money form or money name of the labour materialised in a commodity. Money therefore has no price. And price is a purely ideal or mental, not a real or bodily, form.

Function 2.—The second function of money is to serve as a standard of price. Here follows one of those comparisons that are so frequent with Marx, and are of such incalculable value to the student. In this case, the comparison is between money fulfilling the function of a measure of value, and money fulfilling the function of a standard of price. Let us call these (1) measure of value; (2) standard of price.

Comparison.—(*a*) As (1), money is the general equivalent; as (2), money is a fixed weight of metal.

(*b*) As (1), it converts the values of all commodities into prices, *i.e.* into imaginary quantities of gold; as (2), it measures these quantities of gold.

(*c*) As (1), it measures the value of commodities; as (2), it measures quantities of gold in terms of a unit quantity of gold, say £1.

Change in the Value of Gold.—A change in the value of gold does not affect either of these first two functions. As to (1), no matter how the value of gold may change, the ratio between the values of different quantities of gold remains constant. As to (2), no matter how the value of gold may change, the change affects all commodities simultaneously, and does not therefore affect their relative value.

Discrepancy.—After a time, a discrepancy arises between the current money names of the various weights of the money metal, and the actual weights that these names originally represented.

Causes.—This discrepancy is due to (*a*) the importation of foreign money with foreign names into an imperfectly developed country, *e.g.* Rome. (*b*) The ousting of the less valuable metal, *e.g.* silver, by the more valuable, *e.g.* gold. The pound was the money name of an actual pound weight of silver. It is now applied to a sovereign. (*c*) The debasing of the currency.

Function 3.—The standard of money, therefore, in the end, is regulated by law. A legally fixed quantity, *e.g.* one ounce of gold, is legally divided and subdivided into aliquot parts, and these are legally named (shilling, penny, etc.). As prices are now expressed in the names of coins, we have now a third function of money. It now serves as money of account.

SECTION 2.—THE MEDIUM OF CIRCULATION.

Function 4.—*(a)* The metamorphoses of commodities.

C - M - C'.—In exchange there is a double metamorphosis. A commodity (C), is turned into money (M), and this money is reconverted into another commodity (C'). C - M - C' is therefore the general formula for the exchange of commodities.

C - M.—C - M, the first phase of this, is, upon the part of the owner of C, sale. But upon the part of the owner of M, it is purchase. The owner of M generally owns it as the result of an earlier transaction, in which some other commodity, (C''), was exchanged for this M, so that the first phase, (C - M), in the metamorphosis of a commodity, is also the second phase in the metamorphosis of some other commodity (C''). C'' has earlier undergone the transformation C'' - M, and now undergoes the re-transformation, M - C.

M—C'.—The second phase is, upon the part of the

owner of C (the original commodity), purchase. But upon the part of the owner of C' it is a sale, and a sale that will later be succeeded by another purchase of another commodity, say C'''. So that the second phase, M—C', in the metamorphosis of a commodity, is also the first phase in the metamorphosis of C' from the commodity form to the money form, the beginning of a new metamorphosis, C' - M - C'''.

Terms and People.—For the complete metamorphosis of a commodity there are necessary four terms and three people. The terms are (1) money; (2) commodity; (3) owner of money; (4) owner of commodity. The people are (1) the buyer in the first transaction; (2) the seller in the first transaction, who is also the buyer in the second, and who meets in the second transaction (3) a new commodity owner.

Circulation of Commodities.—C - M - C' is a circuit. But this circuit is interwoven with the circuit C'' - M- C' of another commodity. And this latter circuit is again interwoven with that of yet another commodity, C''' - M - C . The sum total of all the different circuits of all commodities is the circulation of commodities.

Difference between this and Direct Barter.—This circulation of commodities differs from direct barter, with which it is often confused by the ordinary political economist, in that (1) the owners of C and C' do not mutually exchange their commodities; (2)

the process does not end when the use-values have changed places and hands; (3) the process bursts through all restrictions of time, place, and persons, imposed by direct barter.

(*b*) The currency of money.

Currency of Money.—By the phrase, "the currency of money," is meant the course it takes in going from hand to hand.

A Monotony.—The movement of the commodity is in a circuit, C - M - C. But the movement of money is a monotony. It goes farther and farther away from its starting-point. Its course is a monotony from buyer to seller. In the sphere of circulation the commodity appears and disappears. Money is always within that sphere.

$Q=\frac{S}{N}$.—The quantity (Q) of money functioning as the circulating medium within the sphere of circulation during a given time is the sum (S) of the prices of all the commodities concerned, divided by the number (N) of changes of place made in the time by coins of the same denomination, *e.g.* sovereigns. $(Q=\frac{S}{N})$.

$Q=\frac{S}{V}$.—Or, the quantity of money functioning as the circulating medium within the sphere of circulation during a given time is the sum (S) of the prices of all the commodities concerned, divided by the average velocity of the course of money. $(Q=\frac{S}{V})$.

(*c*) Coin and symbols of value.

Coin.—That money takes the shape of coin springs from its fourth function as the means of circulation.

Symbols.—Coins wear and tear. Thus, from the outset their nominal and their real weight begin to dissever; the distinction between them as bits of metal and as coins with a function appears. And this implies the possibility of their replacement by other symbols. Satellites, *e.g.* in the shape of copper coin, take their place where coins pass quickly from hand to hand. Paper money, *e.g.* such as bank notes, without value itself, can yet serve only symbolically. This paper—the outcome of the function of money as a means of circulation—must not be confused with cheques (credit money), the outcome of the function of money as a means of payment, a function yet to be considered. Paper money is therefore a token representing gold in its function as a means of circulation. It expresses symbolically the value of commodities, as the equivalent quantity of gold expresses ideally the value of commodities.

Law.—The law of paper money is that the issue of paper money must not exceed the amount of gold that would circulate if there were no paper money.

SECTION 3.—MONEY.

Summary.—We have seen that the general equivalent, *e.g.* gold, functions as (1) a measure of value; (2) a standard of price; (3) money of account—in all these cases it is the ideal money commodity—and (4) a circulating medium, in which function it is capable of representation by symbols, such as copper coins or bank notes.

Function 5.—The general equivalent functions as money, in the restricted sense, when it has to be actually present in a transaction, and when, either in its own actual person or by representative, *e.g.* cheques, it is the sole form of value, the sole form of existence of exchange-value in opposition to use-value, represented by all other commodities.

m.—When the general equivalent (M) thus functions as money in the restricted sense, it may be represented by *m.*

(*a*) Hoarding.

M to m.—When a sale is not at once followed by a purchase, M passes from its condition of coin (p. 28) into that of money, *m.*

Hoarding of m.—In the earlier stages of the circulation of commodities, a desire, a passion arises to retain the result of the first metamorphosis, C - M. Hence hoarding. As in these earlier stages, only surplus use-values are turned into *m*, the hoards become the social expression of superfluity of riches. As production and circulation of commodities develop, the producer must have in hand more and more *m.* The æsthetic form of this hoarding of M is the possession of gold and silver articles.

(*b*) Means of payment.

Function 6.—When, as the circulation of commodities develops, time elapses between parting with the commodity and the realising of its price, when C-M becomes C—M, the general equivalent has a new function. It is now the means of payment, *m*'. Buyer and seller are now debtor and creditor. M now not only functions as a measure of value, but also as an ideal means of purchase. It is only promised by the debtor, and yet it effects a change of place of the commodity. It only becomes *m*', the actual means of payment, at the end of a certain time, entering into circulation after C has left the sphere of circulation.

From this function of M as *m*', of the general equivalent as a means of payment, spring credit-money, cheques, bills, etc.

(*c* Universal money.

Bullion.—When money leaves the home sphere of circulation it is extradited, it loses all local forms of standard of prices, coin, etc., and is simply in its general form,—bullion. It is again and finally the social incarnation of human labour in the abstract. In the home sphere of circulation, only one commodity becomes money; in the world-market, two (gold and silver) become money.

Three Functions.—Universal money has three functions. (1) It is the universal means of payment (*m*'), as in the settling of international balances; (2)

it is the universal means of buying, when the customary equilibrium in the international exchange of products is disturbed ; (3) it is the universal embodiment of social wealth, as in the case of subsidies, war loans, etc.

Movement of Gold and Silver.—The movement of gold and silver is double. (1) From the source where they are found to the world-market ; (2) from country to country, from one national sphere of circulation to another.

PART 1.—THE TRANSFORMATION OF MONEY (*M*) INTO CAPITAL (*C*).

CHAPTER IV.—THE GENERAL FORMULA FOR CAPITAL.

Preliminary Stages.—The production of commodities, their circulation, its developed form, commerce, the world-embracing form of commerce dating from the sixteenth century, lead up to the capitalistic system.

M - C - M'.—Money *(m)*, the final product of the circulation of commodities, is the first form of Capital. The formula C - M - C' is that of the circulation of commodities. But this formula also implies M - C - M', the formula for capitalistic circulation. All money describing this latter circle is, potentially, capital.

Comparison.—A very important comparison is then instituted between these two formulæ; C - M - C' (circulation of commodities) and M - C - M' (capitalistic circulation). In comparing them let us call the former C - M - C' (1); and the latter M - C - M' (2).

Resemblances.—The two formulæ, (1) and (2), are alike in three points.

(*a*) In each, there are two phases, a sale and a purchase.

(*b*) In each, commodities and money are concerned

(*c*) In each, three people are concerned.

Differences.—The two formulæ, (1) and (2), differ in twelve points.

(*a*) (1) begins with a purchase and ends with a sale; (2) begins with a sale and ends with a purchase.

(*b*) In (1), M is the intermediary; in (2), C is the intermediary.

(*c*) In (1), the two end terms are commodities; in (2), the two end terms are money.

(*d*) In (1), money is spent; in (2), money is advanced.

(*e*) In (1), the same piece of money changes place twice; in (2), the same commodity changes place twice.

(*f*) In (1), the same piece of money passes from one hand to another; in (2), the same piece of money returns to the same hand.

(*g*) In (1), if a reflux of money to the same starting-point does occur, the series, C - M - C', starts again; in (2), the series M - C - M' is incomplete until such reflux of money to the starting-point does occur.

(*h*) The aim of (1) is use-value; the aim of (2) is exchange-value.

(*i*) In (1), the two end terms have different qualities; in (2), the two end terms have different quantities.

$M' = M + \Delta M$, *i.e.* M' is equal to the original sum advanced, M, + an increase, ΔM. This ΔM is *surplus-value.*

(*k*) In (1), the values of C and C' are normally equivalent; in (2), the values of M and M' are normally not equivalent.

(*l*) In (1), the process ends in the consumption of C; in (2), the process is endless. M' becomes a new M.

(*m*) The circulation of commodities is a means to an end, that end being the consumption of use-values.

The circulation of money as capital is an end in itself.

Aim of Capitalist.—The aim of the capitalist is not a use-value, but ΔM, *i.e.* surplus-value.

General Formula.—This general formula M - C - M' covers not only merchants' capital, but industrial capital also. In interest-bearing capital the formula M - C - M' is shortened into M - M'.

CHAPTER V.—CONTRADICTIONS IN THE GENERAL FORMULA OF CAPITAL.

Source of Δ *M.*—This chapter is devoted to the demonstration of the fact that surplus-value cannot be created by the simple circulation of commodities. What is the source of surplus-value?

Not in formulæ 1 - 4.—In all the transactions represented by the formulæ (1) xA = yB (p. 6); (2) xA = yB = zC = etc. (p. 10);

$$(3) \quad \left.\begin{matrix} yB \\ vC \\ xD \end{matrix}\right\} \text{each} = zA \text{ (p. 11)};$$

(4) C - M - C' (p. 25)—there is an exchange of equivalents. There is no alteration of value, no creation of surplus-value. The ordinary political economist thinks that the source of surplus - value is in C - M - C' and in its developed form—commerce. He falls into this error because he confuses use-value and exchange-value.

Arguments Against.—Like Darwin, Marx always exhausts the arguments against his own position.

That Non-Equivalents are Exchanged.—Assume (1) that non-equivalents are exchanged in the formula C - M - C'. But the seller who has gained or lost, say 10 per cent., upon the actual value of his commodity (C), now becomes in his turn a buyer, and straightway loses or gains that 10 per cent. The final result is as if all had exchanged equivalents and there is no creation of surplus-value.

That Δ *M is Paid by the Consumers.*—Assume (2) that surplus-value is paid by the consumers of commodities. But the consumer either is or represents a producer, and the case is therefore the same as the one just considered.

A Consuming Non-Producing Class.—Assume (3) the existence of a class that only buys and does not sell; only consumes and does not produce. But selling commodities above their value to such a class is only taking back a part of the money previously given to that class.

That A gets the Better of B.—Assume (4) that the seller gets the better of the bargain with the buyer. But the total amount of value is just the same as before, although its distribution may be changed.

Conclusion.—The conclusion is therefore that circulation or exchange of commodities does not beget surplus-value. Something therefore must take place in the background that is not apparent in the circulation itself.

Problem.—The problem still is—how to account for the origin of capital upon the supposition that the starting-point of the conversion of money into capital is the exchange of equivalents, and that prices are regulated by the average price (*i.e.* ultimately by the value) of commodities.

CHAPTER VI.—THE BUYING AND SELLING OF LABOUR-POWER.

Not in M.—Still seeking the origin of surplus-value (Δ M), it is not in the money itself. For money in its functions of means of purchase and means of payment only realises prices. And in its function as money in the restricted sense (*m*, p. 29), *i.e.* as cash, it is value petrified and invariable.

Nor in C - M'.—Nor can the change take place in the phase C - M' of the circle M - C - M', for in this the commodity simply passes from its bodily to its money form.

Must be in C and in its Use-Value.—The change must therefore take place in the phase M - C of the circle M-C-M' and in C, since, as we have seen, it cannot take place in M. But the change cannot be in the value of C, since equivalents are exchanged. We are therefore forced to the conclusion that the change ending in the formation of Δ M (surplus-value) takes place in the use-value of C, *i.e.* in the consumption of the commodity.

The Special Commodity.—A commodity has therefore to be found, whose use-value has the property of being a source of value, whose consumption creates value. The commodity is labour-power.

Labour-Power.—Labour-power is the sum total of the mental and physical faculties of a human being that can be exercised when the human being produces a use-value. Labour-power must not be confused with labour, as it often is by the political economists. Labour is the realisation of labour-power, and results only when the commodity, labour-power, is consumed.

The Free Labourer.—The free labourer must be (1) personally free to sell his labour-power for a definite time only, and not forever and a day; (2) free from any other commodity, *i.e.* without any of the means of subsistence or the means of production. He must therefore be obliged to sell his only commodity—labour-power.

Essentials to Capitalistic Production.—Capitalistic production has no law-of-nature basis. It is a stage in historical evolution. Its essentials are (1) that use-value and exchange-value are distinct; (2) that the stages of (*a*) barter and (*b*) the circulation of commodities are past; (3) that the capitalist, the possessor of the means of subsistence and production, meets in the market the free labourer only possessing his labour-power.

Value of Labour-Power.—The value of labour-power, as the value of all commodities, is determined by the labour-time necessary for its production and re-production, *i.e.* by the labour-time necessary for the production of the means of subsistence of the labourer.

Means of Subsistence.—These means of subsistence for the labourer are food, fuel, clothes, housing, furniture, for himself and his children (the commodity, labour-power, must be continuous upon the market), education.

Labour-Power Advanced to the Capitalist.—The use-value of the commodity, labour-power, does not, at once upon the conclusion of the contract, pass into the hands of the buyer. Hence C—M (see p. 30). The money of the capitalist that is to be paid for the wage-labour becomes means of payment (*m'*, p. 30) And the use-value of the commodity, labour-power, is advanced to the capitalist.

To the Factory.—Leaving now the sphere of the circulation of commodities, we are to pass into the factory, and study the production of the commodities themselves. This part, this chapter, and this section end with a singularly powerful passage. The long, close chain of reasoning is followed by an outburst of great strength. The philosopher becomes the great writer.

PART III.—THE PRODUCTION OF ABSOLUTE SURPLUS-VALUE.

CHAPTER VII.—The Labour-Process and the Process of Producing Surplus-Value.

SECTION 1.—THE LABOUR-PROCESS OR THE PRODUCTION OF USE-VALUES.

Labour.—Labour-power in use is labour. The capitalist sets the labourer to produce a particular use-value.

Factors of a Labour-Process.—The three factors of a labour-process are (1) man's activity, *i.e.* work itself; (2) the object upon which it works; (3) the instruments with which it works. These three factors let us henceforth denote respectively by 1, 2, 3.

Object.—2 may be immediately provided by Nature, as soil. Let us call these natural objects upon which 1 works, 2*a*. Or 2 may be raw material, *i.e.* natural objects that have been worked upon by human labour. Let us call raw material, 2*b*.

Extractive Industry.—When the object upon which 1 is working is only 2*a* and not 2*b*, the industry is called extractive. Mining is an example.

Raw Material.—2*b* may be either the substance of the ultimate product, as when cotton is turned into yarn, or auxiliary. These auxiliary raw materials are (*a*) consumed, *e.g.* gas; (*b*) united with the chief substance, *e.g.* dyes; (*c*) help to carry on the work, *e.g.* the acid in candle-making.

Instruments.—3 are the things that man interposes between himself and 2 as conductors of energy from him to 2. The earth itself, furnishing a *locus standi* to the labourer, buildings, canals, streets, tools, are examples.

A Product.—A use-value, and therefore a product (let us call it 4), are formed when 1 works upon and modifies 2 by aid of 3.

Its Fate.—The fates of a product (4) are (*a*) immediate consumption by individuals; (*b*) ultimate consumption by individuals; (*c*) to become the raw material (2*b*) for one particular product, *e.g.* cotton for yarn; (*d*) to become the raw material for more than one product, *e.g.* corn for millers, cattle-breeders, etc.; (*e*) to become an instrument of labour (3); (*f*) to become both 2*b* and 3, *e.g.* fat cattle, which also produce manure.

Means of Production.—The objects of labour (2) and the instruments of labour (3) are means of production, *mp.* The man's activity does not come under the head of *means* of production.

Consumption.—Labour is an act of consumption of the commodity labour-power—the realising of its use-value. Individual consumption occurs when the products are used for the subsistence of the individual. Productive consumption occurs when the product is to be worked upon with a view to producing yet another product, not the bodily frame of the consumer.

Table.—A tabular arrangement of the factors of

Factors
- **Work** **1**
- *mp.*
  - Objects
    - Natural....... 2*a*
    - Raw Material 2*b*
  - Instruments **3**

Labour process ending in Product (4), whose fate is
- **Individual Consumption** ....
  - Immediate.
  - Ultimate.
- Productive Consumption
  - **2*b* or 3**
    - **Raw Material 2*b***
      - For one Product.
      - More than one.
    - Instrument of labour 3.
  - **2*b* and 3. Raw Material and Instrument.**

the labour-process, and of the fates of its products, may be of service to the student here.

Transition to the Capitalistic-Process.—When the labour-process becomes the capitalistic-process, two things occur: (*a*) the labourer works under the control of the capitalist; (*b*) the product (4) becomes the property of the capitalist.

SECTION 2.—PRODUCTION OF SURPLUS-VALUE.

Object of the Capitalist.—The product that becomes the property of the capitalist is a use-value. But use-values are only desired by the capitalist because they are exchange-value carriers. The capitalist has in view the production of a use-value that has an exchange-value (*i.e.* the production of a commodity), and the production of a commodity whose value is greater than the sum of the values of the labour-power, the object, the instruments (1, 2, 3) used in its production.

Work and Labour.—A commodity is a use-value and a value. The process of producing a commodity is a labour-process creating use-value, and also a process of creating value. The former process is work; the latter process is labour. This latter process—the creation of value—is now the only one under consideration. The labour now under consideration is therefore only abstract human labour, differing in no way qualitatively, but only quantitatively.

An Important Passage.—Hereupon follows, perhaps, the most important passage in "Capital." It is one of the passages most frequently read and quoted. But, of course, for its full comprehension, all that has gone before is necessary. In analysing it, as in reading it, we must remember that the figures chosen are arbitrary, but that this fact in no wise affects the argument based upon them.

Theoretical Case.—Cotton (2*b*, p. 41) is to be turned into yarn (the product). Let the value of one hour's labour be 6d. Let 10 lbs. of cotton, worth say 10s., be turned in six hours into 10 lbs. of yarn, worth 1s. 6d. a lb. Let the wear and tear of the spindles and other instruments (3, p. 41) amount to 2s. So that, without reckoning the labour, we have in the yarn a value of 10s. + 2s. = 12s., transferred from 2*b* and 3, to 4. Six hours of labour spent in turning 2*b* into 4, at 6d. an hour, cost 3s. The total value now embodied in 4 = 12s. + 3s. = 15s. And 10 lbs. of yarn at 1s. 6d. a lb. are worth 15s. There is no gain: there is no surplus-value.

Outcry of the Capitalist. — The usual arguments of the capitalist against this unsatisfactory condition of things are then given by Marx and answered.

The capitalist will buy on the market and not manufacture commodities. But if all the capitalists do this, where is the market?

The capitalist must be paid for his abstinence. But he has the yarn.

The capitalist supplied the labourer with 2 and 3. But the labourer has supplied 1, and the value of 2 and 3 are transferred to and embodied in 4, which is now the property of the capitalist.

The capitalist has given his time. But the labourer has given his.

The Three Values of Labour-Power.—What really occurs in the factory, however, is this. In the labour-power of the labourer, past labour is embodied, and there is also a living labour, resulting from the consumption of that labour-power. There is a daily cost of maintaining labour-power; there is a daily expenditure of labour-power. The former cost determines the exchange-value of the labour-power; the latter cost determines its use-value. Therefore the value of the labour-power is one thing and the value it creates in the labour-process is another thing. The labourer realises the exchange-value of his commodity and parts with its use-value to the capitalist. The essence of the whole transaction is that labour-power is the source, not only of value, but of more value than the labour-power has itself.

Real Case.—Therefore the capitalist has ready for the labourer in the factory the means of production necessary, not for working six hours, but for working, say, twelve. Instead of 10 lbs. of cotton there are 20 lbs. Now, let us balance up accounts. The 20 lbs. of cotton represent 20s. of crystallised human labour. The wear and tear of the spindles and other instruments, for twelve hours, represent 4s. of crystallised human labour. The labour-power is paid, as before, 3s. If it is paid 6s., the former condition of the theoretical case again obtains, and there is no creation of surplus-value.

Expenditure, 20s. + 4s. + 3s. = 27s.

But the capitalist has now 20 lbs. of yarn at 1s. 6d.

Receipts, 1s. 6d. × 20 = 30s.

He has a surplus-value of 30s. − 27s. = 3s., or $\frac{1}{9}$ of the value (27s.) of the factors 1, 2, 3 necessary to the production of the yarn.

Degree, Not Kind.—The production of surplus-value is therefore only due to an extension of the production of value beyond the point at which the value of the expended labour-power (1) has been replaced. Commercial production becomes capitalistic production, when production is not merely a labour-process and a value-creating process, but also a surplus-value creating process.

Skilled Labour.—Whether the labour is skilled or unskilled does not affect the question. Surplus-value results, not from a qualitative difference in the labour-power (this only affects the use-value of the product), but from a quantitative difference. That portion of his labour by which a skilled workman replaces the value of his own labour-power does not differ, quantitatively, from that portion by which he creates surplus-value.

CHAPTER VIII.—Constant Capital and Variable Capital.

mp.—The three factors of the labour-process are, as we have seen: (1) labour; (2) the object upon which the labour is expended; 2*a* natural objects, 2*b* raw material; (3) instruments. And 2 and 3 are, collectively, the means of production. Let us denote them (as above, p. 41) by *mp.*

Transference and Creation of Value.—The value of *mp* is preserved in the labour-process, and is transferred to the product. Thus the labourer (*a*) transfers the value of *mp* and (*b*) adds new value. He does the former (*a*) by virtue of his particular kind of labour (spinning, weaving, etc.); he does the latter (*b*) by virtue of his labour being also labour in the abstract and functioning for a certain time. By the quality of his labour he transfers the value of *mp.* By the quantity of his labour he adds new value.

mp Not the Source of Surplus-Value.—The value of *mp* transferred to the product is never greater than the value they themselves lose in the transference. The means of production are not the source of surplus-value. The whole of their value ultimately reappears in the product.

Constant Capital.—In the product we have the value of the labour-power consumed, and also the surplus-value (Δ M) that the labour-power has created. Surplus-value is the difference between the value of means of production and labour-power taken together, and the value of the product. As Δ M does not arise from *mp*, that part of capital which is represented by *mp* is constant capital. Let us denote it by *cc*.

Variable Capital.—And the part of capital represented by labour-power (from which surplus-value can arise) is variable capital. Let us denote this by *vc*.

"Constant" is Not the Same as Fixed.—Fixed capital, in the ordinary sense, is only a part of *cc*, as Marx uses the phrase. Fixed capital is the more or less durable form,—represented by machinery, buildings, etc.,—as opposed to circulating capital, *e.g.* raw material. The constant capital (*cc*) of Marx includes both fixed and circulating capital.

CHAPTER IX.—THE RATE OF SURPLUS-VALUE.

SECTION 1.—THE DEGREE OF EXPLOITATION OF LABOUR-POWER.

$C = cc + vc$.—The total capital advanced is made up of the constant capital and the variable capital. $C = cc + vc$. Marx writes $C = c + v$. I have ventured to alter the form of the formula in my notes for two reasons. Students often use v for value (they would do better, I think, to use V); and cc and vc tell by the additional c more than c and v alone.

s.—The total value of the product $= cc + vc + \Delta M$ (surplus-value). Let us henceforth denote surplus-value by s. And let V denote the total value of the product. Then, as we have seen, $V = cc + vc + s$; the value actually created is $vc + s$. The value of the means of production, transferred only, is cc.

$\frac{s}{vc}$.—The relative increase in the value of vc is the rate of surplus-value. It is expressed, as all ratios are expressed, by dividing the one quantity (the surplus-value) by the other (the variable capital). Therefore the expression for the rate of surplus-value is $\frac{s}{vc}$.

$\frac{s.l.t.}{n.l.t.}$—Again, the labourer during the first part of the day produces only the value of his labour-power, the value of his means of subsistence. This portion of the working-day is necessary labour-time, necessary for the production of his means of subsistence. After the expiration of the necessary labour-time, the labourer is creating surplus-value. This portion of the working-day is surplus-labour-time. If we represent necessary labour-time by *n.l.t.* and surplus-labour-time by *s.l.t.*, we have now two expressions for the rate of surplus-value, $\frac{s}{vc}$ or $\frac{s.l.t}{n.l.t.}$

Ordinary Method of Calculation.—$\frac{s}{vc}$ is therefore an expression for the degree of exploitation of labour-power by capital. The ordinary calculation of the political economist is based upon $\frac{s}{C}$—*i.e.*, the ratio of the surplus-value created to the whole of the capital advanced. The proper calculation is based upon $\frac{s}{vc}$—a much larger rate.

SECTION 2.—THE REPRESENTATION OF THE COMPONENTS (*cc, vc, s*) OF THE VALUE (V) OF THE PRODUCT BY CORRESPONDING PROPORTIONAL PARTS OF THE PRODUCT.

Concrete Example.—A concrete example is taken. Let us suppose that V (total value of product) = 30s., made up of *cc* (24s.), *vc* (3s.), *s* (3s). Suppose (p. 45) that the product is 20 lbs. of yarn. Of these 20 lbs. $\frac{24}{30}$ represent *cc*; $\frac{3}{30}$ represent *vc*; $\frac{3}{30}$ represent *s*. Therefore, of the 20 lbs., $\frac{5}{6}$ or 16 lbs. represent *cc*; $\frac{1}{10}$ or

2 lbs. represent *vc*; $\frac{1}{10}$ or 2 lbs. represent *s*. The total product consists of (1) a part representing the labour contained in *cc* (2) a part representing the labour contained in *vc* or necessary labour; (3) a part representing the labour contained in *s* or surplus-value.

SECTION 3.

The "Last Hour."—Is devoted to showing the fallacy of Nassau Senior's contention that all the profit is made in the last hour of the working-day.

SECTION 4.—SURPLUS-PRODUCE.

Surplus-Produce.—Surplus-produce is the portion of the product that represents surplus-value. In the concrete example given above, the surplus-produce is 2 lbs. of yarn.

Its Ratio.—Here also the relative quantity of surplus-produce must be calculated, not as the political economists calculate it, in relation to the whole of the product, but in relation to that part of the whole product in which is incorporated necessary labour. In the concrete example given above, the ratio of the surplus-product, as well as that of the surplus-value, is not $\frac{2}{20}$ or $\frac{1}{10}$ or 10 per cent., but $\frac{2}{2}$ or 1 or 100 per cent.

CHAPTER X.—The Working-Day.

SECTION 1.—THE LIMITS OF THE WORKING-DAY.

a—*b*—*c*. *a*—*b*——*c*. *a*—*b*———*c*.

In the key-note, we have represented three working-days of different lengths. In all of them the part *ab* (necessary labour-time) is, of course, of the same length, say 6 hours. The part *bc* (surplus-labour-time) varies, representing in the three cases, respectively, say 1, 3, 5 hours.

$\frac{bc}{ab}$.—The rate of surplus-value, $\frac{s}{vc}$ or $\frac{s.l.t.}{n.l.t.}$, here becomes $\frac{bc}{ab}$. The part *ab* is determinate. The part *bc* is not.

Limits.—The minimum limit of the working-day is *ab*. The maximum is, of course, not twenty-four hours for the individual labourer, as the labourer must satisfy his desire for rest and other physical needs.

Labourer to Capitalist.—Under this section occurs the famous appeal from the labourer to the capitalist for a normal working-day,—a passage of wonderful dramatic strength.

"The commodity that I have sold to you differs from the crowd of other commodities in that its use creates value, and a value greater than its own. That is why you bought it. That which on your side appears a spontaneous expansion of capital, is on mine extra expenditure of labour-power. You and I know on the market only one law, that of the exchange of commodities. And the consumption of the commodity belongs not to the seller who parts with it, but to the buyer who requires it. To you, therefore, belongs the use of my daily labour-power. But by means of the price that you pay for it each day, I must be able to reproduce it daily, and to sell it again. Apart from natural exhaustion through age, &c., I must be able on the morrow to work with the same normal amount of force, health and freshness as to-day. You preach to me constantly the gospel of 'saving,' and 'abstinence.' Good! I will, like a sensible, saving owner, husband my whole wealth, labour-power, and abstain from all foolish waste of it. I will each day spend, set in motion, put into action, only as much of it as is compatible with its normal duration and healthy development. By an unlimited extension of the working-day, you may in one day use up a quantity of labour-power greater than I can restore in three. What you gain in labour I lose in substance. The use of my labour-power and the spoliation of it are quite different things. If the average time that (doing a reasonable amount of work) an average labourer can live is 30 years, the value of my labour-power, which you pay me from day to day, is $\frac{1}{365} \times \frac{1}{30}$ or $\frac{1}{10950}$ of its total value. But if you consume it in 10 years, you pay me daily $\frac{1}{10950}$ instead of $\frac{1}{36\,50}$ of its total value, *i.e* only $\frac{1}{3}$ of its daily value, and you rob me, therefore every day of $\frac{2}{3}$ of the value of my commodity. You pay me for one day's labour-power, whilst you use that of 3 days. That is against our contract and the law of exchanges. I demand, therefore, a working-day of normal length, and I demand it without any appeal to your heart, for in money matters sentiment is out of place. You may be a model citizen, perhaps a member of the Society for the Prevention of Cruelty to Animals, and in the odour of sanctity to boot; but the thing that you represent face to face with me has no heart in its breast. That which seems to throb there is my own heart-beating. I demand the normal working-day, because I, like every other seller, demand the value of my commodity."

SECTION 2.—THE GREED FOR SURPLUS-LABOUR. MANUFACTURER AND BOYARD.

Corvée.—Surplus-labour has not been invented by capital. In Athens, Etruria, Rome, America, Wallachia, it has existed. Marx takes the case of the corvée of the Danubian principalities as an example. By law, 14 days a year of actual labour are to be given to the boyard-master. In practice, these 14 are expanded to 42. Moreover, there is jobagie, or 14 days of extraordinary service to the boyard. 42 + 14 = 56. And as there are only some 140 working-days in the

Wallachian year, the ratio of the corvée, or of the given labour (56 days) to the necessary labour (140—56=84 days), is $\frac{56}{84}=\frac{2}{3}=66\frac{2}{3}$ per cent.

SECTION 3.—BRANCHES OF ENGLISH INDUSTRY WITHOUT LEGAL LIMITS TO EXPLOITATION.

Condition of Workers.—Here are given a series of terrible quotations as to the conditions of the workers in branches of production not at the time of writing under legal restriction as to hours of work. Obviously, it is not necessary to give these in a note-book like this. But certainly they should be read by every one who wishes to strengthen his scientific socialism by emotional socialism. They occur upon pp. 227-241 of the English translation.

SECTION 4.—DAY AND NIGHT-WORK. THE RELAY SYSTEM.

Night Labour. The Relay System.—Here are given another series, not less terrible, of quotations from the reports of the Children's Employment Commission, as to the employment of women and children at night, and as to the devices by which the capitalist tries to appropriate the whole of the twenty-four hours of the working-day. The chief of these devices is the relay system or the alternation of shifts of workers, so that the works are kept going day and night. That which was written as to Section 3 applies to Section 4 (pp. 241-248).

SECTION 5.—THE STRUGGLE FOR A NORMAL WORKING-DAY. COMPULSORY LAWS FOR THE EXTENSION OF THE WORKING-DAY FROM THE MIDDLE OF THE FOURTEENTH TO THE END OF THE SEVENTEENTH CENTURY.

Deterioration.—The limits of the working-day (*ac*, p. 54) are not determined by the normal maintenance of the labourer's labour-power, but by the greatest possible daily expenditure of that labour-power. Hence deterioration, premature exhaustion, and even death of the labour-power. And this deterioration of the industrial town population is only retarded by the constant absorption of the country people into the towns.

Two Opposed Tendencies.—The establishment of the normal working-day in England shows two opposed tendencies. (*a*) That of the English Labour Statutes from about 1350, to lengthen the working-day; (*b*) that of the Factory Acts from 1833 onwards, to shorten the working-day.

(*a*) English Labour Statutes.

1349.—(1) Statute of Labourers, Edward III., 1349. This fixed the limit of the working-day for all artificers and field labourers, from March to September, as from 5 A.M. to 7 P.M., with 3½ hours for meals—in all, 10½ hours; from October to February, from 5 A.M until dark, with 3½ hours for meals.

1496.—(2) Statute of Labourers, Henry VIII., 1496. Repeats that of 1349.

1562.—(3) Statute of Elizabeth, 1562. This leaves the limits of the working-day untouched, but shortens down the 3½ meal-hours to 2½ in the summer, and 2 in the winter.

SECTION 6. — THE STRUGGLE FOR THE NORMAL WORKING-DAY. COMPULSORY LIMITATION BY LAW OF THE WORKING-TIME. (*b*) THE ENGLISH FACTORY ACTS, 1833 to 1864.

Beginning of the Struggle.—The introduction of machinery into England led to the breaking down of all bounds of morals, nature, age, sex, day, night. The struggle for the legalised normal working-day set in.

1802-1833.—Between the years 1802 and 1833, five labour laws were passed; but, as no money was voted by Parliament for the carrying of them out, they were dead letters. Up to the year 1833, children and young persons (by the latter phrase is always meant those from 13 to 18 years of age) were worked *ad libitum.*

1833.—The Factory Act of 1833 dealt with cotton, wool, flax, silk factories. It fixed the working-day from 5.30 A.M. to 8.30 P.M. = 15 hours. But no young person to work individually more than 12 hours, or at night, and every young person to have 1½ hours for meals. Children from 9 to 13 only to work 8 hours, and not at night. Children under 9 not to be employed at all.

Relays.—In order that the shortening of the hours of young persons and children might not limit the working-day of the men, the masters introduced the system of relays or double sets of children, one set working from 5.30 A.M. to 1.30 P.M., and the other set from 1.30 P.M. to 8.30 P.M.

The Gilding of the Pill.—To gild the pill for the masters, the Act of 1833 was not to come into force until March 1, 1834. Also from that date to March 1, 1835, the limit age of the children who were only to work 8 hours was to be 11 years; from March 1, 1835, to March 1, 1836, the limit was to be 12 years; and the limit, 13 years, was only to come into force after this last date.

Agitation of the Masters.—As this date, March 1, 1836, approached, the masters agitated so violently that the Government, in 1835, actually proposed to make the limit age for a child, not 13 but 12. Popular opinion was, however, too strong, and the 1833 Act held for ten years.

1833-1844.—During these years the masters, working against the Corn-Laws, needed the help of the working-class, and therefore went with them in their agitation for the Ten Hours Bill. This led to the Act of 1844.

1844.—By this, women were placed upon the same footing as young persons—12 hours a day and no night-work. For the first time, the labour of adults was "interfered with" by Act of Parliament. The working-time of children was reduced from 8 to 7 or to 6½ hours. A consequence of this was the indirect limitation of the working-day of men, as in most factories the men could not work without the co-operation of the women, young persons, and children. Upon the other hand, the lower limit of age for children was reduced from 9 to 8 years.

1847.—During the time from 1844 to 1847, the working-class found allies in the Tories; hence the Act of June 8, 1847. This shortened the working-day for young persons and women. From July 1, 1847, the day was to be 11 hours as against 12 before, and from May 1, 1848, it was to be 10 hours.

Master-Dodges.—In answer to this, the masters, 1, tried to hinder the Act from coming into force in 1848. The condition of the men was very bad, in consequence of the crisis of 1846-7. The masters therefore first reduced wages 10 per cent. Next, when the 11 hours came into force, they reduced them 8⅓ per cent. Next, when the 10 hours came into force, they reduced them 16⅔ per cent.

2. They got up false petitions.

3. They made use of Press and Parliament in the pretended name of the working-class.

4. They allowed the men to work from 12 to 15 hours, and said the men did this from choice.

Thanks to Leonard Horner and the other factory inspectors who exposed all these dodges, the Act came into force.

1848.—Then came 1848, with the failure of the Chartist movement in England, and the insurrections abroad. The capitalists took advantage of the terror of the ruling class, and tried to undo all that had been done between 1833 and 1847.

Master-Tactics.—1. They discharged many of the young persons and women, and restored night-work for the men.

2. They attacked the meal-hours. Why should not the labourer feed at home and not in working-hours?

3. Whilst keeping to the strict letter of the law of 1844 as far as it concerned children, they fixed the time of the children's 6½ hours *after* the young persons and women had finished. Thus they exploited the men for more than 10 hours.

4. With young persons and women they simply broke the law literally.

5. They introduced the shifting system. This had two forms. (*a*) They got the labourer into the factory for a time, sent him out again, called him in, and so on during the 15 hours of the factory-day, never losing hold of him all this time, although his total time of labour might be only 10 hours. (*b*) They

shifted the individual worker from one kind of labour to another, from one factory to another, with, as consequence, insuperable difficulties to the factory inspectors.

Appeal to Law.—These last appealed to the law. But the magistrates on the bench were the very people prosecuted. And upon February 8, 1850, the Court of Exchequer declared that the Act of 1844 contained words that rendered it meaningless.

Results.—The results were practical abolition of the Ten Hours Day, and all the masters going in for the relay system. Upon the other hand, there were meetings of the working-class, warnings from the factory inspectors, grumblings on the part of the masters in country districts who could not find enough people to work the relay system. Final result—the Act of 1850.

1850.—This Act was a compromise. Its provisions for children were the same as those of the Act of 1844. For young persons and women, 10 to $10\frac{1}{2}$ hours a day, with $7\frac{1}{2}$ only on Saturday. The working-time to be between 6 A.M. and 6 P.M. in the summer; between 7 A.M. and 7 P.M. in the winter —$1\frac{1}{2}$ hours for meals. Thus the relay system, so far as the callings named on p. 59 were concerned, was killed.

1853.—As the Act of 1850 did not alter the condition of children under the Act of 1844, the capitalistic device noted under 3, par. 6, p. 62, was still possible. But the Act of 1854 stopped this. It forbade the employment of children in the morning before, and in the evening after, the young persons and women were at work.

Other Industries.—All these Acts, thus far, only affect the four industries, cotton, wool, flax, silk, mentioned on p. 59. But in 1845, the print-workers; in 1860, the dyers and bleachers; in 1861, lace and stocking-makers; in 1863, the makers of earthenware, lucifer matches, percussion caps, cartridges, carpets, etc., open-air bleachers, and bakers came under the Factory Acts.

SECTION 7. — THE STRUGGLE FOR THE NORMAL WORKING-DAY. REACTION OF THE ENGLISH FACTORY ACTS ON OTHER COUNTRIES.

The Succession of Industries.—The passion of capital for the extension of the working-day is first gratified in the industries first revolutionised by water-power, by steam, and by machinery—cotton, wool, flax, silk. In all these, that passion is first restrained by legislation. Later, and by degrees, other branches of industry come under capitalistic exploitation, and therefore later, and by degrees, come under the Factory Acts.

The Succession of Countries.—The process first begins in England, the home of modern industry. France follows slowly, although the twelve hours law that followed in that country upon the Revolution of 1848 recognised the principle of the limitation of all labour, even adult, not, as in England, only legislating for children, young persons, and women. The French law, however, allows of the relay system, and therefore of night-work. In the United States the first fruit of the Civil War was the eight hours agitation.

CHAPTER XI.—RATE AND MASS OF SURPLUS-VALUE.

Mass of s.—The rate of surplus-value $=\frac{s}{vc}$. The mass or quantity of surplus-value extracted by the capitalist from the labourer is now to be considered. Thus far, and now, the value of labour-power and the *n.l.t.* are supposed constant.

$VC = Pn$ (i).—The total variable capital (vc) of the capitalist may be represented as VC. Let the value of one labour-power be P, and let the number of labourers employed by the capitalist be n. Then, $VC = Pn$ (i).

$S = VC \times \frac{s}{vc}$ (ii).—Let S represent the sum total or mass of surplus-value extracted. Then, $S = VC \times \frac{s}{vc}$ (ii). I need hardly point out that VC and vc are numbers, and that there can be no cancelling of the letters of the one against the letters of the other.

$S = Pn \times \frac{s.l.t.}{n.l.t.}$ (iv).—Again, (p. 52) $\frac{s}{vc} = \frac{s.l.t.}{n.l.t.}$ (iii). In equation (ii), *i.e.* $S = VC \times \frac{s}{vc}$, substitute the value of VC in equation (i), and of $\frac{s}{vc}$ in equation (iii), and we have $S = Pn \times \frac{s.l.t.}{n.l.t.}$, or the mass of the surplus-value extracted is equal to the value of the labour-power of one labourer multiplied by the number of labourers, multiplied again by the rate of surplus-value, expressed in the form surplus-labour-time divided by necessary-labour-time.

Equations (ii) *and* (iv).– Looking at equation (ii), $S = VC \times \frac{s}{vc}$ it will be seen, therefore, that diminution in the amount of variable capital (VC) may be compensated by a rise in the rate of surplus-value, or by a rise in the degree of exploitation of labour-power ($\frac{s}{vc}$). And, looking at equation (iv), $S = Pn \times \frac{s.l.t.}{n.l.t.}$, it will be seen that a decrease in the number of labourers (n) may be compensated by a lengthening of the surplus-labour-time, by a lengthening of the working-day. This last lengthening has, of course, a limit.

vc, not cc.—From this it follows that S depends entirely upon the mass of labour that is set in motion, therefore upon P*n*, therefore upon VC. The mass of constant capital (*cc*) that may be employed does not count in the creation of surplus-value. S varies, not as the total capital C, but as VC, the amount of the variable constituent (*vc*) of the total capital C.

The Position.—The capitalist (1) becomes master of the labour-power; (2) sees that it works properly, and with sufficient intensity; (3) compels the labourer to work surplus-labour-time, and to produce surplus-value.

From the point of view of the creation of surplus-value, the labourer does not employ the means of production. The means of production employ the labourer.

PART IV.—PRODUCTION OF RELATIVE SURPLUS-VALUE.

CHAPTER XII.—THE CONCEPT OF RELATIVE SURPLUS-VALUE.

Increased Productiveness.—a———b—c. The problem for the capitalist is to get more surplus-labour-time, and therefore more surplus-value, without lengthening *ac*. The solution is: shorten *ab*, and thus lengthen *bc*. And this is brought about by an increase in the productiveness of labour, *i.e.* by a change in the labour-process, by virtue of which the labour-time necessary to the production of a commodity is lessened.

Absolute and Relative s.—Surplus-value due to the lengthening of *ac*, is absolute surplus-value. Surplus-value due to the shortening of *ab*, as the result of increased productiveness of labour, is relative surplus-value.

"Means" must be Affected.—Increased productiveness of labour, if it is to affect *ab*, must affect the means of subsistence of the labourer or the means of production—numbers **2** and **3** in the labour-process (p. 41).

The Enigma.—Why does the capitalist, whose sole concern is the production, not of use-values but of exchange-values, always try to lower the exchange-value of commodities?

Its Solution.—Relative surplus-value varies *as* the productiveness of labour; the value of commodities varies *inversely as* the productiveness of labour. Increase, therefore, in the productiveness of labour augments the surplus-value in a commodity, and at the same time cheapens the commodity. So the capitalist is anxious to heighten the productiveness of labour, because whilst this certainly cheapens commodities in general, it also cheapens the especial commodity, labour-power, and so increases the relative amount of surplus-value contained in all commodities.

Summary—The object, therefore, of all development in the productiveness of labour for the capitalist, is to shorten *ab*, lengthen *bc*, and get more relative surplus-value.

CHAPTER XIII.—CO-OPERATION.

Meaning of Word.—Co-operation here is not to be confused with the modern co-operative systems. Co-operation here simply means the working together of many labourers under the capitalist.

Quantitative and Qualitative.—The working together of many labourers at the same time, in the same place, is the starting-point of capitalistic production. The difference between this and the handicraft trade of the guilds is, at first, only quantitative. But, following the law of Hegel, the difference soon becomes qualitative.

Economy.—With the simultaneous employment of many labourers, there is economy in the use of the means of production (1) through the general cheapening of commodities and the consequent diminution in the value of labour-power; (2) through the alteration of the ratio ($\frac{s}{C}$). This, let it be noted, is not the rate of surplus-value ($\frac{s}{vc}$), but the ratio of the surplus-value to the total capital advanced.

Collective Labour-power.—Most important in co-operation is that with it comes the creation of a new power,—the collective power of the many. One man in one day, *e.g.*, can make one pair of trousers. Three men in one day can make twelve pairs of trousers. The capitalist pays for the three independent labour-powers. But he never pays for the collective or combined labour-power of the three. To this point of the non-recompense to the labourers of their collective labour-power, and the appropriation of it by the capitalist for nothing, the attention of the student is specially directed.

Gains.—The gains from co-operation are (1) this enormously important new power,—the collective or combined labour-power of the many ; (2) the stimulation of the animal spirits of the labourer working with his fellows; (3) when the kind of work is the same, it can be attacked on all sides at once; (4) if it is not the same, there can be apportionment of the various operations to different individuals ; (5) critical periods, such as harvest-time, can be tided over; (6) extension of space, as in road-making.

Combined Working-Day.—The combined working-day, therefore, produces, relatively to an equal sum of isolated working-days, more use-values.

Stages of Co-operation.—The stages of co-operation are (*a*) that met with in hunting races or the agriculture of Indian communities, where (1) the means of production are held in common ; (2) each individual is part and parcel of his own tribe. (*b*) The sporadic co-operation of ancient times, the middle ages, and modern colonies, dependent upon relations of dominion and slavery. (*c*) Capitalistic co-operation dependent upon free labour.

Stages of Co-operation

- **Means of Production common, tribal**
  - Hunting Races.
  - Agricultural Indian Communities.
- Slavery
  - Ancient.
  - **Mediæval.**
  - **Colonies**
- **Free Labour** …… Capitalistic

CHAPTER XIV.—Division of Labour and Manufacture.

SECTION 1.—THE TWOFOLD ORIGIN OF MANUFACTURE.

Date.—The manufacturing period, as distinct from that of the grand industry which follows it, dates from the middle of the sixteenth to the last third of the eighteenth century.

Synthesis and Analysis.—Manufacture arises in two ways. 1. Synthetic. The assemblage in one workshop, under the capitalist, of many labourers belonging to different handicrafts, through whose hands an article must pass on its way to completion; *e.g.* a coach.

2. Analytic. Division of labour among men all doing the same work originally; *e.g.* pin-making.

Still, thus far, the handicraft is the basis of this form of co-operation. The productive mechanism is men, not, as yet, machinery.

SECTION 2.—THE DETAIL LABOURER AND HIS IMPLEMENTS.

Gains.—The gains are (1) those arising from the general nature of co-operation (p. 71); (2) of time, as the one man is doing one thing and not passing from one occupation to another; (3) improvement of methods; (4) tricks of the trade handed on, and even heredity playing its part; (5) specialisation of tools.

Loss.—Upon the other hand, we must reckon as a negative quantity the lessened interest of the labourer always working at the one kind of work.

SECTION 3.—THE TWO FUNDAMENTAL FORMS OF MANUFACTURE—HETEROGENEOUS AND SERIAL.

The Two Forms.—1. Heterogeneous. The fitting together of partial products made independently; *e.g.* a watch.

2. Serial. Passing through a series of processes; *e.g.* a pin. Here, with many labourers, the detail processes successive in time may become simultaneous in space.

Manufacture and Co-operation. — Manufacture therefore goes farther than simple co-operation.

1. It not only finds the conditions for co-operation ready to hand, but creates them by the sub-division of handicraft labour.

2. Each labourer gives on his product as raw material to the next labourer.

3. Each labourer takes for his labour the socially necessary time, and continuity obtains.

4. Fixed mathematical relations arise, determining the relative number of labourers for each detail operation.

The Collective Labourer.—As manufacture arises in part from the grouping of handicrafts, so manufacture develops into groupings of manufactures. The machinery of the manufacturing period, as distinct from that of the period of grand industry yet to be considered, is the collective labourer.

Unskilled Labour.—Manufacture develops a succession of higher and lower labour-powers, with a succession of higher and lower wages. As there are certain simple operations that any one can do, manufacture begets the unskilled labourer needing no apprenticeship or teaching. With the fall in the value of labour-power caused by this disappearance of apprenticeship, there is a direct increase of surplus-value for the benefit of the capitalist.

SECTION 4.—DIVISION OF LABOUR IN MANUFACTURE, AND DIVISION OF LABOUR IN SOCIETY.

Three Forms of Division of Labour.—(*a*) In general; agriculture, industries, etc.

(*b*) In particular; the divisions of agriculture, of industries, etc.

(*c*) In detail, within the workshop.

Resemblances Between Division of Labour in Manufacture and in Society.—Let us call division of labour in manufacture (1); division of labour in society (2).

(*a*) In both (1) and (2) there are two origins—the synthetic and the analytic. In the synthetic, the cause is exchange between spheres of production originally distinct and independent. In the analytic, the cause is a physiological division of labour due to difference of sex and age within the tribe.

(*b*) For (1), a certain number of simultaneously employed labourers are necessary; for (2), a certain number and density of population are necessary.

(*c*) For (1), production and circulation of commodities are necessary.

And this demands a certain degree of development of (2), to which the colonial system and the opening of world-markets lend themselves.

Differences.—(*a*) In (1), the detail labourer produces no commodity; in (2), the products ultimately are commodities.

(*b*) In (1), there is a sale of the labour-powers of the labourers to one capitalist; in (2), there are purchase and sale of the products of different branches of industry.

(*c*) In (1), there is concentration of the means of production in the hands of one capitalist; in (2), there is dispersion of the means of production among many independent producers of commodities.

(*d*) In (1), the law of proportionality (p. 74) subjects definite numbers of labourers to definite functions; in (2), chance and caprice play parts in distributing the labourers.

(*e*) In (1), there is the undisputed authority of the capitalist; in (2), there are independent commodity-producers and competition.

(*f*) (1) is praised by the bourgeois; (2) is, in its conscious form, condemned by the bourgeois.

(*g*) In (1), there is despotism; in (2), there is anarchy.

(*h*) (1) is a special creation of the capitalistic method of production; (2) is common to many and to different forms of production.

SECTION 5.—THE CAPITALISTIC CHARACTER OF MANUFACTURE.

Increase of Minimum C.—With the necessary increase in the number of labourers (n) under division of labour in manufacture, comes a necessary increase in the amount of *vc*, and also indirectly of *cc*. So that the minimum amount of C that must be in the hands of the individual capitalist increases.

The Separation.—The separation between the labourer and the means of production begins in simple co-operation, develops in manufacture, is completed in modern or grand industry yet to be considered.

The Individual Labourer.—Under manufacture, in order that the collective labourer, and through him capital, may be rich in social productive power, the individual labourer must be poor in individual productive power. Science under manufacture, and later under modern industry, serves the capitalist alone. The labourer undergoes deterioration and degradation, and a special pathology of labour is begotten.

Summary.—Manufacture, therefore, *i.e.* co-operation based upon division of labour, is only a particular form of getting surplus-value, and under it the national wealth, the domination of the capitalist, the productiveness of labour, all increase.

In the manufacturing period the number of unskilled labourers is small, and there is much insubordination of the labourer.

When manufacture produces machines, we pass to modern industry.

CHAPTER XV.—MACHINERY AND MODERN INDUSTRY.

SECTION 1.—THE DEVELOPMENT OF MACHINERY

Effect of Machinery.—Machinery shortens *ab* (in the working-day), lengthens *bc*, produces more relative surplus-value. Under manufacture, already considered, the revolution in the method of production began with labour-power. In modern or grand industry, now to be considered, the revolution in the method of production begins with the instruments of labour.

Machine.—What is the difference between a tool and a machine?

Answers. 1. A tool is a simple machine; a machine is a complex tool.

2. With a tool, the motive-power is man; with a machine, the motive-power is something other than man.

3. The best. A machine is a tool (*c*), plus a motor mechanism (*a*) and a transmitting mechanism (*b*). From *a* through *b* energy is transmitted to *c*. And it is in *c*, the tool, that the change from manufacture to machinery begins.

Motor.—Under the grand industry the labourer

using only one tool is replaced by a machine, when a single *a* sets in motion many *c*. The increase in the number of *c* means more massive *b* and stronger *a*. Man, therefore, is replaced by horse or by wind or by water or finally by steam as the motor.

Factory.—A factory is a workshop in which machinery only is used.

Most Complete Form.—The most complete form of production by machinery is an organised system of machines (*c*), to which motion is communicated through the transmitting mechanism (*b*) from a central automaton (*a*).

Machinery by Machinery.—At first the tools (*a*) are manufactured—made by hand. But later they are made by machinery. With the introduction of the steam-engine as prime mover (*a*), and the discovery of the slide rest, the conditions for the making of machinery by machinery obtained.

SECTION 2.—THE VALUE TRANSFERRED BY MACHINERY TO THE PRODUCT.

Gratuities to the Capitalist.—The capitalist pays nothing for (1) collective labour-power (p. 70); (2) physical forces; (3) scientific laws—the capitalistic appropriation of these three is very different from the personal appropriation of them;—(4) machinery.

Machinery's Value.—Machinery, as *cc*, creates no new value. Its value is transferred to the product.

This value of machinery, transferred to and reappearing in the product, is of much greater quantity than the value of the tools in manufacture.

Total and Transmitted Value.—The value of machinery is transmitted to the products bit by bit. Every product into whose production the machine enters has a fraction only of the total value of the machine transmitted to it. There is a great difference between the total value of a machine and the value transferred from it in a given time to the product. And this difference is much greater in a machine than it is in a tool.

Area of the Product.—The extent to which the transmitted value makes the product dearer depends upon the area of the product. The wider this area, *i.e.* the greater the size or the number of the things produced, the less the amount of value transmitted from the machinery to any given portion of a product or to any one product.

Amount of the Product.—The amount of the product will depend upon the velocity of the working parts of the machine.

Generally.—In the product of machinery, the value due to the instruments of labour increases relatively, but decreases absolutely. Its absolute amount is less, but its amount, relatively to the total value of the product, is more.

Productiveness of a Machine.—The productiveness

of a machine is measured by the amount of human labour-power that it replaces.

Concrete Example.—Suppose a machine costs as much as one year's wages of 150 men whom it displaces, say £3000.

This £3000 does not express the total labour added to the product in one year by the 150 men before the introduction of the machine. It only expresses their necessary labour-time (p. 52) for the year.

On the other hand, the £3000, the money-value of the machine, expresses *all* the labour expended on its production, no matter what was the *n.l.t.* or *s.l.t.*, no matter what was *vc* or what was *s*.

Hence, even if a machine costs as much as the labour-power it displaces, yet the labour embodied in it is less than the labour it replaces.

The Cost to the Capitalist.—From the preceding note, it is clear that it is possible for the difference between the price of machinery and the price of the labour-power it displaces to vary, although the difference between the quantity of labour requisite to produce the machine and the total quantity replaced by it remains constant. And it is the former difference alone that determines the cost, to the capitalist, of producing a commodity.

SECTION 3.—THE PROXIMATE EFFECTS OF MACHINERY ON THE WORKMAN.

(*a*) Appropriation of supplementary labour-power

by capital. The employment of women and children.

Supplementary Labour-Power. — Machinery dispenses with muscular power. The labour of women, young persons, and children is therefore sought for by the capitalist. Every member of the labourer's family is to be enrolled.

Depreciation.—Hence a depreciation in the value of the labourer's labour-power. Machinery thus extends the area of capitalistic exploitation, and at the same time raises the degree of that exploitation.

Change in the Contract.—When the exchange of commodities was taken as the basis of the contract between labourer and capitalist, they met as free persons. But now the capitalist buys children and young persons, and the labourer sells not only his own labour-power, but his wife and child.

Mortality.—A further result is the enormous mortality that, as a consequence, breaks out among children. To the giving of chapter and verse for this, some six pages are devoted.

Resistance Broken Down.—This addition of women, young persons, and children to the ranks of labour ends in the breaking down of that resistance which the men had, during the manufacturing period, offered to the masters.

(*b*) Prolongation of the working-day.

Antithesis.—Machinery is the most powerful means

for increasing the productiveness of labour, *i.e.* for shortening the working-time required for the production of a commodity. But in the hands of capital it becomes the most powerful means for lengthening the working-day.

Reasons.—Machinery creates (*a*) new conditions; (*b*) new motives for capital.

New Conditions. — The implements of labour (3)—(p. 41)—are automatic. So is, to a large extent, the motor-power, the first of the three essentials to machinery, (*a*)—(p. 41). The work is apparently light, and women and children, more pliant and docile than men, are employed.

New Motive No. 1.—The productiveness of a machine varies inversely as the amount of value transferred from it to a given product. The longer its life, the greater the mass of products over which its transmitted value is spread, the less the fraction of that value added to each given product. But this length of life depends upon the length of the working-day.

Machines are worn and torn both from use and non-use (rusting, etc.). And they undergo a moral depreciation, as more and better machines of the same kind come upon the market. Now the shorter the time in which the total value of a machine is reproduced, the less the danger of moral depreciation; and the longer the working-day, the shorter is that time.

New Motive No. 2.—The lengthening of the working-day allows of more production, without any alteration in so much of *cc* as is fixed capital in the ordinary economist's sense, *i.e.* as is laid out in buildings, machinery, and the like.

New Motive No. 3.—When machinery is first introduced into an industry, the labour employed by the owner of the machinery is, at first, of a higher degree and greater efficacy than the average social labour. The capitalist, anxious to make the most of this brief transition period, lengthens the working-day.

New Motive No. 4.—A reference to formula (iv.)—(p. 66), $S = Pn \times \frac{s.l.t.}{n.l.t.}$ shows that for a given S, if the rate of surplus-value is to be increased (n), the number of labourers must be diminished. This diminution in the number of labourers drives the capitalist to lengthen the working-day.

Surplus-Labour Population.—And this setting free of the labourers that are supplanted by the machinery gives rise to the surplus-labour population, whose significance is considered later.

(*c*) Intensification of labour.

Reaction and Its Consequence.—The immoderate lengthening of the working-day leads to a reaction and to the fixing the length of that day by law. And this, in its turn, leads to intensification of labour. Labour now has not only a measure of its extension—

duration, but a measure of its intensity—condensation.

Subjective and Objective Conditions.—The shortening of the working-day creates the subjective conditions for intensification of labour, by enabling the labourer to exert more strength in a given time. Machinery becomes the objective means. (*a*) Machinery is improved in its motor (1), (p. 41), in its transmitting mechanism (2), in its tools (3). Its speed is increased. (*b*) The labourer has more machinery to look after.

Examples.—On pp. 409-417, Marx gives quotations from the reports of factory inspectors and other sources, proving that upon the shortening of the working-days there followed intensification of labour. And this not only in the industries under the Acts. In potteries and other industries where machinery plays little or no part, the shortening of the working-day increases wonderfully the regularity, uniformity, order, continuity, and energy of the labour.

After the Twelve Hours.—The quotations range first over the twelve years from 1832-1844 (see pp. 59-61). So great had the intensification of labour become by 1844, that even the great and good factory inspector, Leonard Horner, actually thought that further intensification was impossible. He under-estimated the elasticity of machinery and of man's labour-power.

After the Ten Hours.—But after 1847, when the

ten hours working-day came in, the quotations tell the same tale of yet further intensification.

Masters' Gain.—And how, with the more intense exploitation of labour-power, the wealth of the masters increased, is shown by the fact that from 1838 to 1850 (twelve years), the average proportional increase in English cotton and other factories was 32 per cent., while from 1850 to 1856 (six years) it was 86 per cent.

Prophecy.—A principle in science is firmly established when a prophecy based upon it proves true. Let the student, knowing what is at the present time the working-class question most in the air, note Marx' words written in 1867: "There cannot be the slightest doubt that the tendency that urges capital, so soon as a prolongation of the hours of labour is once for all forbidden, to compensate itself by a systematic heightening of the intensity of labour, and to convert every improvement in machinery into a more perfect means of exhausting the workmen, must soon lead to a state of things in which a reduction of the hours of labour will again be inevitable."

SECTION 4.—THE FACTORY.

Ure's Definitions.—Ure defines a factory (1) as "combined co-operation of many orders of workpeople,—adult and young,—attending with assiduous skill a system of productive machines continuously impelled by a central power." This definition is applicable to every possible employment of machinery on a large scale.

Or (2) as "a vast automaton composed of various mechanical and intellectual organs, acting in uninterrupted concert for the production of a common object, all of them being subordinate to a self-regulated moving force." This definition is applicable to the use of machinery by capital, and therefore to the modern factory system.

Equalising Tendency.—In place of the gradations of specialised workmen under manufacture, we have under machinery a tendency to reduce to the same level all the work done by those attending to the machines.

Simple Co-operation.—Such division of labour as does obtain in the factory is a distribution of workmen among specialised machines, and of masses of workmen, not organised in groups, among the departments of the factory. The co-operation is therefore only simple.

Workmen.—There are two chief groups. (1) Workmen actually employed on the machines; (2) attendants, mainly children Aggregated to, but distinct from, the factory operative class, is the small number of people that look after the machinery as a whole and repair it—engineers, mechanics, etc.

Specialisation Vanishes.—Machinery does away

with the annexation of a particular man to a particular function, and does away with any special class of operatives.

Comparison between Manufacture and Machinery.—In manufacture, the workman uses a tool. In machinery, the workman is used by a machine.

In manufacture, the movements of the tool proceed from him. In machinery, he follows the movements of the machine.

In manufacture, he is part of a living mechanism. In machinery, he is the living appendage of a lifeless mechanism.

For the Workman.—Exhaustion of the nervous system; monotony; freedom of bodily and mental activity lost; barracks discipline; a factory code; fines; deductions from wages; disease and danger.

SECTION 5.—THE STRIFE BETWEEN WORKMAN AND MACHINE.

Contests.—The contest between capitalist and labourer dates back to the origin of capital, and goes on through the manufacturing period. But the contest between the machine (embodied capital) and the labourer begins under machinery.

Examples.—A number of examples are given. The ribbon-loom in Germany and Holland, and the conflicts to which it—the precursor of the mule and the power-loom, and of the industrial revolution of the eighteenth century—gave rise. The wind saw-mill in London (1630); the wool-shearing machine (1758); the scribbling-mills and carding-engines; the Luddite riots.

Change of Attack.—At first, the workers attacked the material instruments of production. Now, as they are learning to distinguish between machinery and the employment of machinery by capital, their attack is being transferred to the capitalistic method of production as a whole.

Stages Leading up to this Conflict.—(1) The labourer sells his labour-power as a commodity; (2) division of labour specialises this labour-power, reducing it to skill in the use of a particular tool; (3) this tool becomes part of a machine; (4) the use-value and then the exchange-value of the labourer's labour-power vanishes; (5) he becomes superfluous, and goes to the wall, or floods the more easily accessible branches of industry, swamping the labour market and lowering the price of the labour-power.

Misery, Chronic or Acute.—If machinery seizes upon an industry by degrees, the resulting misery to the operatives competing against it is chronic. If machinery seizes upon an industry rapidly, the resulting misery to the operatives competing against it is acute. And, as machinery is continually seizing upon new fields of production, its so-called "temporary" effects are really permanent.

New or Improved Machinery.—The antagonism between the machine and the labourer comes out most strongly when new machinery begins to compete with manufacture. But every improvement in an established machine brings out the antagonism again.

A Weapon Also.—Machinery is not only a competitor. It is the most powerful of weapons on the side of the autocracy of capital.

SECTION 6.—THE THEORY OF COMPENSATION AS REGARDS THE WORK-PEOPLE DISPLACED BY MACHINERY.

Compensation Theory.—The bourgeois economists represented by the Mills, contend that all machinery which displaces workmen sets free an amount of capital sufficient to employ the workmen it displaces.

Concrete Example.—100 men are employed at a wage of £30 a year, *vc*=£3000; *cc*, say, also £3000. Now, assume that by £1500 worth of machinery 50 of the men are displaced. All that happens is that now *vc*=£1500 (50×£30), and *cc*=£4500 (£3000 +£1500). No capital is set free; only £1500 of *vc* are now *cc*.

Even if the machinery only cost £1000, and not £1500, *cc* is now £4000, and there are £500 of *vc* set free. But this £500 cannot compensate the 50 men displaced, only at most one-third of their number.

Makers of the Machinery.—Even if the making of

the new machinery employed as many men as the machinery displaced, and that permanently (two quite impossible suppositions), that would be no compensation to the men that are displaced.

What is Really Set Free.—What *is* set free is the £1500 worth of means of subsistence of the 50 men displaced. The men are discharged, and can no longer get at their means of subsistence, which are, as far as they are concerned, "free." But this £1500 worth of means of subsistence was never capital that was being expanded by the workmen now discharged. The £1500 represented part of the products produced in the year by the 50 discharged men, which they received as wages in money, not in kind, and with which they bought means of subsistence. These means, therefore, were to them, not capital, but commodities; in respect to these means of subsistence, the men were not wage-labourers, but buyers.

Real Facts.—The labourers are thrown upon the labour market, adding to the number at the disposal of the capitalist. If they *do* find some other employment, *new* and additional capital is necessary to form the *vc* necessary for their wages.

Antitheses.—Machinery, considered alone, shortens the hours of labour; under capital, lengthens them.

Machinery, considered alone, lightens labour; under capital, intensifies it.

Machinery, considered alone, is a victory of man

over Nature; under capital, is the enslavement of man to Nature.

Machinery, considered alone, increases the wealth of the producers; under capital, makes them paupers.

Law.—If the total quantity of the article produced by machinery is equal to the total quantity of the article previously produced by manufacture, the total labour expended is diminished. As a matter of fact, the total quantity of the article produced by machinery, with fewer workmen, far exceeds the total quantity of the hand-made article displaced.

Indirect Effects.—As the use of machinery extends in a given industry, production is increased in the industries that furnish that industry with the means of production (2 and 3, p. 41).

As the use of machinery extends in preliminary or intermediate stages of production, there is more "yield" in those stages, and more demand for labour in the branches of industry supplied by the produce of the machines.

As machinery, with the aid of fewer people, increases the mass of products, social production increases in diversity, the production of luxuries increases, the carrying trades increase and diversify, new branches of production (*e.g.* railways and telegraphs) appear, and more and more of the working-class are employed unproductively, as, *e.g.*, domestic servants.

SECTION 7.—REPULSION AND ATTRACTION OF WORK-PEOPLE BY THE FACTORY SYSTEM. CRISES IN THE COTTON TRADE.

Relative and Absolute Decrease.—Occasionally an extension of the factory system may be accompanied, not only by the inevitable relative decrease, but by an absolute decrease in the number of labourers employed. Thus, from 1860 to 1865, the increase in looms, in all the factories in a particular district, was 11 per cent.; the increase in spindles, 3 per cent.; in engine-power, 3 per cent.; and the decrease in persons employed was 5½ per cent.

Again, an increase in the number of hands employed may be only apparent, owing to the annexation of allied trades to factories already established.

Again, a relative decrease may be accompanied with actual increase.

Concrete Example.—Suppose, under manufacture, C=£500 (weekly), of which £200 is *cc*, and £300 *vc*—wages, say, £1 a man. After machinery has replaced manufacture, suppose that *cc* becomes £400, and *vc* only £100. Two-thirds of the 300 men, therefore, are displaced, and only 100 left.

Now, assume that the business grows, and that C=£2000, *i.e.* four times as much as before. 400 men will now be employed, an increase of 100 over the original number. But relatively, *i.e.* in proportion to

C, the diminution = 800; for, in the old condition of things, £2000 C would have employed not 400, but 1200 men.

First and Later Periods of Introduction of Machinery.—The first period is a decisive moment on account of the great profits made. Capital is attracted into the favoured sphere of production. When once, however, the general modern industry conditions are established, there is an elasticity about this means of production, only checked by the supply of the raw material (2*b*, p. 41) and the getting rid of the product (4). 2*b*, however, is met with in increased supplies: foreign markets are conquered; emigration, colonisation, and international division of labour set in.

Industrial Cycle.—This elasticity leads to over-production, and then stagnation. The life of modern industry is a series of periods of moderate activity, prosperity, over-production, crises, stagnation. The cotton industry in England from 1770 to 1863 is then taken as an example of this. From 1770 to 1815, the period of monopoly—five years of crisis, five years of stagnation. From 1815 to 1846, when competition with Europe and America sets in—nine years of depression and stagnation. From 1846 to 1863—nineteen years of depression and stagnation.

Cotton Famine.—This was, to some extent, advantageous to the masters. The small ones were swallowed up by the large ones. Most of the mills only worked part time. Inferior cotton being used, the wages of the people who were paid by piecework fell. From these wages fines were exacted, many of them on account of defects in the finished article, due to the inferior cotton. The master, when a landlord, took his rent out of the wages first. Prostitutes increased in number.

SECTION 8.—REVOLUTION EFFECTED IN MANUFACTURE, HANDICRAFTS, AND DOMESTIC INDUSTRY, BY MODERN INDUSTRY.

(*a*) Overthrow of co-operation based on handicraft, and of manufacture based on the division of labour.

Examples.—Of the former, the mowing-machine, replacing co-operation among mowers.

Of the latter, the needle-making machine. One man in Adam Smith's time made 4800 needles a week. One woman or girl can superintend machines making 3,000,000 needles a week.

Transition Cases.—A single machine replacing either of the above, may, for a time, serve as the basis of a handicraft industry. Or an industry may be for a time carried on upon a small scale by means of mechanical power, as in the case of the "cottage-factories" of Coventry in their hopeless twelve years' struggle against the factory proper.

(*b*) Reaction of the factory system on manufacture and domestic industries.

On Manufacture.—Production in all branches of industry not only extends (quantitative change), but alters its character (qualitative). And there is a change in the composition of the collective labourer, since the basis now of the division of labour is the cheap labour of women, children, and the "unskilled."

On Domestic Industries.—Besides the operatives in the factory, capital commands those working for it in their own homes or workshops. Exploitation here is still worse; for (1) the power of resistance of the labourers lessens with their dissemination: (2) middlemen appear; (3) there is competition with the factory; (4) space, light, ventilation, are wanting; (5) employment is irregular; (6) competition amongst the "domestic" workers is at its maximum.

(*c*) Modern manufacture.

Examples.—This section is taken up with examples in illustration of the principles laid down in *a* and *b*, and in the preceding chapter. They are taken from the Children's Employment Commission Report, the Report on the Rag Trade, and the Public Health Report of Dr. Simon.

(*d*) Modern domestic industry.

Examples.—Here again are a number of most appalling statistics and facts, again from the Children's Employment Commission. Once for all let me note that I do not here, or at any other part of this analysis, intend to quote these quotations. They can be, and they should be, read by every one; but the giving them does not come within the scope of this work. They are nevertheless of the greatest possible value to the student, as a confirmation of the position of Marx, and as a stimulus to action.

(*e*) Passage of modern manufacture and domestic industry into modern mechanical industry. The hastening of this revolution by the application of the Factory Acts to those industries.

Stages.—Cheapening of labour-power. Cheapening of commodities. Capitalistic exploitation. Encounter of all these with natural, impassable obstacles. Introduction of machinery. Absorption of manufactures and domestic industries into the factory.

Production of Wearing Apparel.—Marx takes as illustration the production of wearing apparel. In 1861, in England and Wales, 1,024,277 persons were employed as (1) workers in manufactories; (2) small master handicraftsmen, working for the manufactories; (3) domestic workers. The manufactories (see 1) allowed (2) and (3) to continue, with a minimum wage and a maximum working-time.

Sewing-Machine.—The critical point is reached; the natural, impassable obstacles are encountered. The sewing-machine is introduced.

Effect on Workers.—Wages of (2) sink. Women

and girls work the machine at a higher wage than (3). They destroy the men's monopoly of the heavy work, and drive away from the lighter work old women and very young children.

Transition Forms.—These vary greatly. In dress-making (simple co-operation), the machine is, at first, only a new factor in that manufacture. In tailoring, etc., the forms are mixed,—factory system proper; middlemen "sweaters"; families; central capitalist with many machines, who employs the domestic workers.

Causes of the Conversion.—The conversion of all these to the factory system proper is led up to by (1) the tendency to concentrate under one roof and management the scattered branches of a trade; (2) the convenience of having the preparatory needlework, etc., done on the premises; (3) the expropriation of the domestic workers; (4) the glut of machine-made articles, forcing the domestic workers to sell their machines; (5) the over-production of machines compelling their owners to let them out on hire; (6) the substitution of the steam-engine for man. In this, as in most industries, handicrafts, manufacture, domestic industry pass into the factory system.

Factory Acts Help.—This spontaneous industrial revolution is artificially helped by the Factory Acts. They lead to greater concentration of *mp* (p. 42), and greater concentration of the labourers. These, at the same time, compel greater outlay of capital, and so kill the small master and concentrate capital.

Two Essentials for the Factory System.—Certainty in the result, *i.e.* the certainty of producing in a given time a given quantity of commodities, is an essential condition for the existence of the factory system. So is the possibility of the interruption of the work at the statutory pauses in the working-day, without harming the product.

Impediments to the Regulation of the Hours of Labour.—(1) The "impossibilities" of the masters. These always vanish under compulsory legislation.

2. The irregular habits of the labourers.

3. Anarchy in production.

4. Periodic changes in the industrial cycle (p. 95); special fluctuations in the markets; "seasons."

5. Customs of the trade.

Answers.—From the reports of the Children's Employment Committee, it is proved that (1) "impossibilities" vanish before larger buildings, more machinery, more labourers, and the alterations in the method of production and distribution that result from these.

(2) and (3). That the mass of labour is spread more evenly over the whole year.

(3) and (4). That the caprices of "fashion" are checked, and that the development of the means of communication gets rid of the technical basis of season-work.

SECTION 9.—THE FACTORY ACTS. SANITARY AND EDUCATION CLAUSES OF THE SAME. THEIR GENERAL EXTENSION IN ENGLAND.

Clauses Not Affecting Hours—Sanitary.—(*a*) Sanitary. These are limited to provisions for white-washing walls, insuring cleanliness in other matters, ventilation, protection against dangerous machinery.

The Nature of Capitalistic Production.—The mere fact that such clauses are necessary in an Act of Parliament, shows the character of capital. The 500 cubic feet of air for each person (it ought to be 800) cannot be wrung from the masters by the inspectors. In one mill near Cork, between 1852 and 1856, there were six fatal and sixty ordinary accidents, all preventable by the outlay of a few shillings.

Education Clauses.—(*b*) Education. The factory children, although only at school half the time of the others, are fresher, readier, more willing than, learn as quickly and as much as, the others. In these clauses lies the germ of the education of the future, which will for every child combine productive labour, instruction, and gymnastics.

Immanent Antagonism.—The immanent antagonism between the manufacturing division of labour and the methods of modern industry, shows itself in many ways. Notably in the fact that many children are chained to some one simple manipulation, *e.g.* the printers' boys who put paper under, or take printed sheets from, the machines, and are later on fit for nothing.

Technology.—Modern industry, analysing every process of production, founds the science of technology. This discovers the few main fundamental forms of motion that make up every productive action of man. Just as Mechanics works out the few main fundamental simple machines that make up all machinery.

Result of the Antagonism.—Modern industry necessitates variation of labour and universal mobility of the labourer. On the other hand (see last note but one) it reproduces and petrifies the old division of labour. This contradiction between technical necessities and the social character of modern industry renders the position of the labourer insecure, and will lead to the ending of the capitalistic system. "The historical development of the antagonisms immanent in a given form of production is the only way in which that form of production can be dissolved and a new form established."

Extension of the Factory Acts to "Home."—The regulation of "home-labour" by legislation was, at first, an attack upon parental authority. But even Parliament was forced to recognise that modern industry, overturning the economical foundation upon which the traditional family was based, had loosened all the traditional family ties.

The Real Position.—It was not that the misuse of parental authority created the capitalistic exploitation of the labour of children. It was the capitalistic exploitation which had caused the misuse of parental authority. The Teutonic-Christian form of the family is no more final than the Roman, Greek, or Eastern form.

Generalisation of the Factory Acts.—The extension of the Factory Acts to other industries than the original four (p. 59) was an inevitable necessity in the historical development of modern industry. The two things that finally decide are (1) that capital, legally controlled at one point, compensates itself with more and more recklessness at others; (2) that the capitalists cry out for equality in competition, *i.e.* for equal legal restraint upon all exploitation of labour.

1867.—Hence, August 15, 1867, the Factory Acts Extension Act, covering eleven industries, whenever 50 or more persons were employed 100 or more days in the year in those industries.

August 21, 1867, the Workshops Regulation Act dealing with small industries (handicrafts and workshops) was passed.

Drawbacks.—The Factory Acts Extension Act was vitiated by vicious exceptions and cowardly compromises with the masters.

The Workshops Regulation Act was a dead letter in the hands of the municipal and local authorities to whom it was intrusted. And when, in 1871, Parliament took the execution of it from them and gave it to the factory inspectors, only eight more inspectors were added to the already under-manned staff, although over 100,000 workshops and 300 brickworks were added to their labours of supervision.

Mining Industry.—The mining industry differs from others, in that here the landlord and capitalist interest are working together.

1842.—The Inquiry Commission of 1840 led to the Mining Act of 1842, by which women and children under 10 were not to be employed underground.

1860.—The Mines Inspecting Act of this year provided for the inspection of mines by public officers duly appointed, and for the non-employment of boys between 10 and 12, unless they had a school certificate or attended school for a certain number of hours. This Act remained a dead letter.

1866 Report.—From the Report of the Select Committee on Mines, 1866, with its cross-examination of the witnesses as if they were in an English Court of Justice, and the Commissioners were impudent and shameless barristers (compare our Labour Commission of 1891), Marx gives another awful series of quotations under the heads: (1) employment in mines of boys of 10 years and upwards; (2) education; (3) employment of women; (4) coroners' inquests; (5) false weights and measures; (6) inspection of mines.

Insufficiency of Inspectors.—In the year 1865 there were in Great Britain 3217 coal mines and 12 inspectors. A Yorkshire mine-owner calculated that, putting on one side their office work, each mine might be visited by an inspector once in ten years.

1872.—A very defective Act, regulating the hours labour of children employed in mines, and making the capitalist to some extent responsible for "accidents."

Agriculture.—In 1867 a Royal Commission was appointed to enquire into the condition of children, young persons, and women employed in agriculture. It published reports, and abortive attempts were made to extend the Factory Acts to agriculture.

Summary.—The extension of factory legislation to all trades is inevitable. But that means the concentration of capital in a few hands, and the factory system universal. This generalisation of capital generalises the opposition to capital. In the individual workshop, order; in production generally, anarchy. The small and domestic industries vanish. The surplus-labour population has no outlet. The material conditions ripen. The social combination of the processes of production ripens. The antagonism in the capitalist method of production ripens. The old society explodes, and the new society rises from its ashes.

SECTION 10.—MODERN INDUSTRY AND AGRICULTURE.

Effect of Machinery.—The use of machinery in agriculture is for the most part free from the injurious physical effect it has in the factory. But its action in displacing the labourer is more intense.

Annihilation of the Peasant.—In agriculture, modern industry has a more revolutionary effect than even in factories. It annihilates the peasant and replaces him by the wage-labourer.

Agriculture and Industry.—The old bond between these is broken by capitalistic production. Agriculture and industry, thus separated and developing, later on undergo a higher synthesis.

Martyrdom of the Producer.—In agriculture, as in industry, the machine employs and enslaves the producer. And in this case, the dispersion of the labourer over wide areas lessens his power of resistance. Further, the soil, as well as the labourer, is robbed.

PART V.—THE PRODUCTION OF ABSOLUTE AND OF RELATIVE SURPLUS-VALUE.

CHAPTER XVI.—Absolute and Relative Surplus-Value.

Labour-Process in the Abstract.—Considering the labour-process in the abstract, from the point of view of its result, apart from historical forms (1), p. 41, is productive labour; (2) and (3) are *mp.* This method of determining when (1) is productive labour, does not hold when we consider the labour-process in the concrete, under the historical form of capitalistic production.

The Collective and the Individual Labourer.—The above definition of productive labour holds, under capitalistic production, for the collective labourer. But it no longer holds for the individual labourer.

As capitalistic production is essentially the production of surplus-value, the individual labourer is only productive when he produces surplus-value for the capitalist.

Absolute Surplus-Value.—The prolongation of the

working-day beyond *ab* (p. 41)—the necessary labour-time—leads to the production of relative surplus-value. This is the basis of the capitalistic system, and the starting-point for the production of relative surplus-value.

Relative.—This last, which presupposes the capitalistic method of production, revolutionises the technical processes of labour, and revolutionises society with its development and the development of the capitalistic system. The formal subjection of labour to capital is replaced by the real subjection of labour to capital.

Transition Forms.—Forms in which as yet surplus-labour is not extorted by direct compulsion, are the independent handicraftsmen, the old-fashioned agriculturists, and the domestic industries.

Productiveness of Labour.—If the labourer wants all his time to produce his means of subsistence, he has no *s.l.t.* (no surplus-labour-time), and there is no capitalist. To have *s.l.t.* there must be a certain degree of productiveness of labour; and this is a gift, not of Nature, but of historical development.

Physical Fetters.—Apart from historical development, the productiveness of labour is fettered by physical conditions. (1) The nature of man himself; (2) natural conditions, these falling into two sets: (*a*) natural wealth in means of subsistence; (*b*) natural wealth in means of production.

s.l.t.—Surplus-labour-time is greater in proportion as necessary labour-time is less. And this is less, as the fertility of the soil and the favourable nature of the climate are greater, and the number of natural wants of the individual are smaller.

The Temperate Zone.—The quantity of *s.l.t.* varies with the physical conditions of labour, especially with the fertility of the soil. But as the capitalistic mode of production is based on man's power over Nature, it is not where Nature is strongest that the capitalistic method obtains most readily. The temperate zone is the hot-bed of capital.

Nature.—Nature, then, explains nothing of the "innate faculty of labour to produce surplus-value." It only explains the longer or shorter length of *ab*, and therefore directly or indirectly the length of *ac*.

Mercantilists.—The mercantile school derived the excess of price over cost of production of the product from the act of exchange and the selling of the product above its value.

Ricardo.—Ricardo never troubles himself about the origin of surplus-value. To him it is inherent in capitalistic production, and capitalistic production is the natural form of social production. Productiveness of labour, to him, is not the cause of surplus-value, but only determines the magnitude of surplus-value.

His School.—His followers, however, have proclaimed the productiveness of labour as the cause of profit (they mean surplus-value). But they did not solve the problem.

J. S. Mill.—Mill repeats the errors of Ricardo's popularisers, and then confounds the duration of labour-time with the duration of its products. According to him, there will always be profits, even without the buying and selling of labour-power.

Profits.—Profits are not calculated, as Mill thinks, on the *vc*, as the rate of surplus-value is, but on C *i.e.* on the total capital advanced (v. i. p. 113).

CHAPTER XVII.—Changes of Magnitude in the Price of Labour-Power and in Surplus-Value.

Value of Labour-Power.—The value of labour-power depends upon three things: (*a*) the value of the means of subsistence; (*b*) the expense of developing the labour-power, varying with the mode of production; (*c*) the natural diversity of the labour-power of men, women, young persons, children.

Assumptions.—In this chapter the factors *b* and *c* are neglected. It is further assumed that commodities are sold at their value, and that the price of labour-power rises occasionally above, but never falls below, its value.

Generally.—The magnitude of the surplus-value, and the magnitude of the price of labour-power, depend on (*a*) the length of the working-day (*ac*, p. 54); denote this by *l*. (*b*) The intensity of labour, whereby a given quantity of labour is expended in a given time; denote this by *i*. (*c*) The productiveness of labour, whereby more or less product is produced by the same quantity of labour; denote this by *p*. Marx then proceeds to investigate the chief variations that can occur in these three factors, *l*, *i*, *p*.

I. l and i constant; p variable.

Law 1.—A working-day of given length (l) produces the same amount of value, no matter how p may vary. If p varies, more or less products will result, and the price of each product will fall or rise, but the amount of value spread over the greater or less number of products will remain the same.

Law 2.—Surplus-value varies directly as p ($\propto p$). But the value of labour-power varies inversely as p ($\propto \frac{1}{p}$). Hence an increase in p causes a rise in surplus-value,—a fall in the value of labour-power; a diminution in p causes a fall in surplus-value,—a rise in the value of labour-power.

Although the *amount* in change in the magnitude of the surplus-value and of the magnitude of the value of labour-power must be the same, the *proportion* of the change is not necessarily the same, and can only be the same when $n.l.t. = s.l.t.$

Law 3.—Variation in surplus-value, when p varies, is the effect and never the cause of variation in the value of labour-power.

Sequence.—The sequence is: (*a*) change in p; (*b*) change in value of labour-power; (*c*) change in surplus-value.

Means of Subsistence.—The value of labour-power is determined by the value of the means of subsistence, and this value changes with p.

Ricardo.—Ricardo was the first to formulate laws

1, 2, 3. But (*a*) he held that *l* and *i* never varied, and that *p* alone varied. (*b*) He, like the other economists, does not investigate surplus-value as a whole, independently of its forms, rent, interest, profit, etc.

Surplus-Value and Profit.—As a consequence of *b*, Ricardo, like Mill (p. 110), confuses surplus-value with one of its divisions—profit. Really the rate of surplus-value is $\frac{s}{v}$ (p. 51). The rate of profit is much less, as it is $\frac{s}{c}$.

II. *l* and *p* constant; *i* variable.

Increased i.—More products *and* more value. The price of the individual products, therefore, does not, in this case, fall, but rises.

And the surplus-value and the value of labour-power may now vary directly as one another.

The Products Affected.—When *p* varies, there is no change in the value of labour-power, and therefore in the amount of surplus-value, unless the products of the industries affected are the means of subsistence of the labourer (see 4th note above). But when *i* varies, there is a change in the magnitude of the value created, no matter what the product is.

III. *p* and *i* constant; *l* variable.

Law 1.—The amount of value created depends on the length of *ac*, *i.e.* of the working-day.

Law 2.—Every change in the relation between the magnitudes of surplus-value, and of the value of labour-power, arises from a change in the absolute magnitude of the surplus-labour, and therefore of the surplus-value (a change in *bc*, the *s.l.t.* or surplus-labour-time of the working-day).

Law 3.—The absolute value of labour-power can change only in consequence of the reaction exercised by the prolongation of *bc* upon the wear and tear of labour-power. Variation in the absolute value of labour-power under variation of *l*, is the effect, and never the cause, of variation in the magnitude of surplus-value. Compare this with Law 3 under I.

l Less.—*n.l.t.* is not changed. Nor is the value of labour-power. But *s.l.t.* is shortened. Hence the absolute and (since *n.l.t.* is not changed) the relative magnitude of the surplus-value falls.

Arguments Against Lessening l.—The capitalist can only save himself, if these conditions obtain, by lowering the price of labour-power and reducing wages. And this is his chief argument against shortening the working-day. But the shortening of the working-day never takes place under these conditions. Rise in *p* and *i* always precedes or immediately follows such shortening.

l More.—*n.l.t.* is not changed. Nor is the value of labour-power. But *s.l.t.* is lengthened. Hence the absolute and (since *n.l.t.* is not changed) the relative magnitude of surplus-value rises, and the relative magnitude of the value of labour-power falls.

IV. Simultaneous variations in *l*, *p*, and *i*.

Many Combinations.—Clearly, the possible combinations here are very many, according to the number of the three factors varying, according as they vary in one direction or the other. With the help of the laws given under I., II., III., every possible case can be worked out. Marx only takes two important ones.

Case 1. *p* less and *l* more.

Industries Concerned.—In speaking of less *p*, only the industries whose products determine the value of labour-power—are, in a word, means of subsistence—enter into the calculation (note 5, p. 112).

Example.—(i) *ac* = 12 hours = 6s.; *n.l.t.*, say, = 6 hours; *s.l.t.* = 6 hours. Absolute magnitude of surplus-value = 3s. Relative magnitude to the value of labour-power as 1 : 1.

(ii) Now, let *p* lessen until the value of the labour-power rises from 3s. to 4s., and *n.l.t.* from 6 hours to 8, and let *ac* lengthen by 2 hours. *n.l.t.* = 8 hours; *s.l.t.* = 6 hours. Absolute magnitude of surplus-value has not changed, is still 3s. But relative magnitude to the value of labour-power is now 3 : 4. Absolute magnitude has not changed; relative magnitude has fallen.

(iii) Again, let *p* and the value of labour-power remain as in (ii), and let *ac* lengthen by 4 hours. *n.l.t.* = 8 hours; *s.l.t.* = 8 hours. Absolute magnitude of surplus-value is 4s. But the relative magnitude to the value of labour-power has not altered from (i). It is still 1 : 1. Relative magnitude has not changed; absolute magnitude has risen.

1799-1815.—Between 1799 and 1815 the price of provisions rose, and there was a nominal rise in wages. There was really a fall in wages as expressed in the necessaries of life. Ricardo thought that a diminution in *p* (of agricultural labour) had led to a fall in the rate of surplus-value. Actually, as *i* and *l* had increased, surplus-value had increased both relatively and absolutely. Hence capital and pauperism grew simultaneously.

Case 2. *i* and *p* more; *l* less.

First Effect.—With more *i* and *p*, a greater mass of products in a given time.

Second Effect.—Shortening of *n.l.t.* or *ab.* Of course if the whole working-day were shortened down to *n.l.t.*—if *ac* became *ab*—there would be no more surplus-value, and the capitalistic system would be at an end. In the communistic system of the future, *n.l.t.* or *ab* will be longer than it is to-day, because (*a*) the notion of means of subsistence will widen; (*b*) part of the *s.l.* (surplus-labour) of to-day (that for reserve funds and accumulation) will then become necessary labour.

Economy.—*p* should increase with the economy of labour. And this latter should include economy, not only of *mp*, but of labour. Capitalistic production enforces economy in individual businesses, but, by its anarchy of competition, begets squandering of *mp* and of labour-power, and creates unnecessary employments.

Spare-Time.—In capitalistic society, spare-time for the classes is required by converting the whole life-time of the masses into labour-time.

In the communistic society, spare-time will be greater as *i* and *p* increase, and as the work is more evenly divided among all able-bodied members of society.

CHAPTER XVIII.—VARIOUS FORMULÆ FOR THE RATE OF SURPLUS-VALUE.

Socialist Formula.—The rate of surplus-value $= \frac{s}{vc} = \frac{s}{\text{value of labour-power}} = \frac{s.l.t.}{n.l.t.}$ (i).

Ordinary Formula.—The rate of surplus-value $= \frac{s.l.t.}{ac} = \frac{s}{\text{value created}} = \frac{\text{surplus product}}{\text{total product}}$ (ii). This formula does not express accurately the rate of surplus-value, the degree of exploitation of labour.

Assume, as before, that $ac = 12$ hours, $n.l.t. = 6$, $s.l.t. = 6$. Then by (i) the real degree of exploitation of labour $= \frac{s.l.t.}{n.l.t.} = \frac{6}{6} = 100$ per cent. But by (ii) the false degree of exploitation of labour $= \frac{s.l.t.}{ac} = \frac{6}{12} = 50$ per cent.

s Can be More than 100 per Cent.—If (ii) were accurate, *s.l.t.* must always be a fraction of *ac*, and the rate of surplus-value could never be 100 per cent. But according to Lavergne, who estimates the capitalist share too low rather than too high, the English agricultural labourer gets only one-fourth of this product, and the capitalist three-fourths. This gives the rate of *s* as 3 : 1, or 300 per cent.

The Deception.—This habit of representing *s* as a fraction of all the value created, conceals the essence of capital, *i.e.* the exchange of *vc* for labour-power, and the shutting out of the labourer from the product.

(iii) *Formula.*—The rate of *s* may be expressed $\frac{s}{\textit{value of labour-power}}$ (i) $= \frac{s.l.}{n.l.} = \frac{\textit{unpaid labour}}{\textit{paid labour}}$ (iii). This last is only a popular form of $\frac{s.l.}{n.l.}$ The capitalist pays for labour-power. He receives the usufruct of that labour-power during the *n.l.t.* (for which he has paid) and during the *s.l.t.* (for which he has not paid).

Capital.—Capital is not only the command over labour. It is essentially the command over unpaid labour.

PART VI.—WAGES.

CHAPTER XIX.—The Transformation of the Value, and therefore the Price of Labour-Power, into Wages.

"*Price of Labour.*"—On the surface, the wage of the labourer appears to be that which it is not—*viz.*, the price of labour. It is really the price of labour-power.

The Real Position.—What the capitalist meets on the market is not labour, but the labourer. The latter sells his labour-power. When his labour begins, it is no longer his.

"*Value of Labour.*"—The expression, "the value of labour," is a purely imaginary one—as imaginary as the value of the earth. It is as different from the value of labour-power, as the work done by a machine is from the machine itself.

Wage Form.—The value of labour-power determines the value of labour, determines its price, determines its wage. But this wage form extinguishes all trace of the division of *ac* into *n.l.t.* and *s.l.t.*, into paid and unpaid labour. All labour appears to be paid. This phenomenal form, "wages," concealing the reality of things, is the basis of (*a*) all the juridical notions of labourer and capitalist; (*b*) all the mystifications of capitalistic production; (*c*) all illusions as to the liberty of this method of production; (*d*) all the apologies of the vulgar economists.

Money.—In the payment of wages, money functions as a means of payment (function 4, p. 30).

Use-Value.—The use-value that the capitalist secures is not the labour-power of the labourer, but its function—some particular kind of labour. But at the same time, this labour is abstract labour as well, and creates value.

The Labourer.—The labourer always, assuming $ac = 12$ hours, gives 12 hours of labour. The value of his labour-power may vary with the value of the means of subsistence; its price may vary with the conditions of demand and supply. Every change in the amount of the equivalent that he may receive as wage is, to him, a change in the value or price of 12 hours' work.

The Capitalist.—The capitalist is only interested in the difference between the price of the labour-power he buys and the value which its function—labour—creates.

Deceptive Phenomena.—Two great classes of phenomena in the actual movement of wages keep up the delusion that it is not the value of labour-power, but the value of its function—labour—that is paid for by wages. (*a*) The change of wages with the length of the working-day; (*b*) the individual difference in the wages of different labourers doing the same work.

As to *a*, we might as well hold that the value of the working of a machine, and not the value of the machine, is paid for, because it costs more to hire it for a week than a day.

As to *b*, under slavery the same difference is found, but does not deceive us. And under slavery, it is clearly labour-power that is sold.

CHAPTER XX.—TIME-WAGES.

Many Forms.—Wages take many forms. Only the two fundamental ones,—time-wage and piece-wage,—to be considered.

Time-Wages.—Time-wages are the converted form under which the value of labour-power presents itself.

Nominal and Real Wages.—The laws given in Chapter XVII. are also the laws of wages. The distinction between the exchange-value of labour-power, and the sum of the necessaries of life into which this value is converted, appears as the distinction between nominal and real wages.

Unit Measure.—The unit measure for time-wages is the price of the working-hour. This is $= \frac{\text{the daily value of labour-power}}{\text{working-day of a given number of hours.}}$

Laws.—Given the quantity of, say, weekly labour, the weekly wages depend on the price of labour. Given the price of labour, the weekly wages depend on the quantity of the weekly labour.

Wages by the Hour.—The unit $\frac{\text{dv of lp}}{\text{wd of a given n of h}}$ loses all meaning as soon as the denominator is indefinite, *i.e.* as soon as the working-day ceases to contain a definite number of hours. The labourer is more than ever at the mercy of the capitalist under this vicious arrangement.

Overtime.—When the price of labour, reckoned per working-hour as above, remaining constant, the working-day is prolonged beyond its usual length, the price of labour may be nominally constant and yet really fall. The habit of "overtime," with a little extra pay, has grown up in certain industries. This extra pay includes unpaid labour, just as the price of the customary hours includes unpaid labour.

Low Wages.—The longer the working-day in any branch of industry, the lower the wages. The lowness of the price of labour acts as a stimulus to the extension of the labour-time. And the extension of the labour-time reacts upon the price of labour, and lowers it.

Competition.—Competition among the labourers enables the capitalist to beat down the price of labour, and the falling price of labour enables him to lengthen the working-time.

Then follows competition among the capitalists. To undersell one another, they leave out from the price of the commodity the unpaid part of the labour-price, making a present of this to the buyer. Next, they leave out from the price of the commodity part of the abnormal surplus-value created by the extension of the working-day. Hence an abnormally low selling-price of the commodity, which henceforward is the basis of a low wage for an excessive working-time.

CHAPTER XXI.—Piece-Wages.

Piece-Wages.—These are only a modified form of time-wages, just as time-wages are only a modified form of the price of labour-power. The modification of form does not alter the essential nature of wages, although this form is more favourable to the capitalist than the other.

Measurements.—If $\frac{s}{vc} = 100$ per cent., we may say under piece-work, that each individual piece is half paid and half unpaid for. The working-time the labourer has expended is now measured by the number of pieces he has produced.

Peculiarities.—1. The quality of the labour is controlled by the work itself, which must be of average perfection. Hence piece-wages are a fruitful source of capitalistic cheating.

2. They furnish the capitalist with an exact measure for *i*.

3. Superintendence of labour becomes in great part superfluous. Domestic industry is favoured. The middleman and the contractor-labourer come in.

4. As it is to the interest of the labourer to strain his utmost, *i* is increased.

5. There is a tendency to raise individual wages above the average, but to lower the average. The week's wage will vary with the individual, and there is competition. This does not, however, alter the general relations between capital and labour. The individual differences balance in the workshop as a whole, and the proportion between wages and surplus-value remains unaltered.

6. Piece-wage is one of the chief supports of working odd hours.

Where General.—In the workshops under the Factory Acts, piece-wages become general, because under the Factory Acts capital can only increase the efficacy of the working-day by increasing *i*.

Variation.—Piece-wages vary inversely as productiveness of labour. They fall as the number of pieces produced in a given time rises, and as the working-time spent on each piece falls.

CHAPTER XXII.—National Difference of Wages.

Factors.—In comparing wages in different nations, all the factors determining changes in the value of labour-power must be considered; price of the means of subsistence, cost of training labourer, women and child-labour, *p*, *l*, and *i*.

The average day-wage for the same trades in different countries must be reduced to a uniform working-day. And piece-wage must be reduced to time-wage.

Average i.—The average intensity of labour varies in different lands. These national averages form a scale whose unit is the average unit of universal labour.

National p and i.—As capitalistic production develops, so do *p* and *i*. Hence in the more developed country the nominal wages are higher. This does not say that the real wages are higher. In England, wages are higher to the labourer, but really lower to the capitalist, than on the Continent.

PART VII.—THE ACCUMULATION OF CAPITAL.

First Steps.—The first step is the conversion of a sum of money into *mp* and labour-power.

The second step, the process of production, is complete when *mp* has been turned into commodities containing surplus-value.

Circulation of Capital.—These commodities are thrown into circulation, sold, their value realised as money, this money again turned into capital.

The Capitalist Producer.—To simplify matters, the industrial capitalist, the producer, is taken as representing not only himself, but all who share the surplus-value among them as rent, interest, profits, etc.

CHAPTER XXIII.—Simple Reproduction.

Production and Reproduction.—Every social process of production is, at the same time, a process of reproduction. The conditions of both are the same and involve the replacing of *mp* by an equal quantity of *mp*. And as production is with us capitalistic, so also is reproduction.

Simple Reproduction.—Simple reproduction takes place when Δ M is a constant, and is spent or consumed by the capitalist as regularly as it is gained.

Production of vc.—The labourer not only produces this Δ M (at present, under simple reproduction, to be consumed by the capitalist), but he produces *vc*, the fund out of which his wages are to come. His labour of last year pays for his labour-power of this year. It is the labourer's own labour, realised in a product, which is advanced to him by the capitalist.

Original Capital Vanishes.—The value of the capital advanced, say £1,000, divided by Δ M annually consumed, say £200, = the number of years (five in this case) in which the original capital vanishes.

When, as must be sooner or later, the original capital is consumed, the value of the capital thereafter in hand is only surplus-value that has been appropriated for nothing.

Mere reproduction, therefore, sooner or later turns all capital into accumulated or surplus-value capital.

Even on the assumption that the original capital was acquired by the personal labour of the capitalist, sooner or later this vanishes and is replaced by the result of unpaid labour.

The Labourer and his Product.—The starting-point of capitalistic production—the separation of the labourer from the product of his labour—is renewed and renewed. The product ceaselessly becomes, not only a commodity, but capital—means of subsistence that buy, means of production that command, the labourer.

Consumption.—When the labour consumes the means of subsistence, that is individual consumption (p. 43). By this, the labourer lives. When the labourer consumes *mp* and turns them into commodities with a higher value than that of the capital advanced, that is productive consumption. By this, the capitalist lives.

Individual Consumption.—Even the individual consumption of the labourer is but the conversion of the means of subsistence into new labour-power, to be exploited by the capitalist. It is a factor of the production and reproduction of capital.

Accumulated Skill.—The reproduction of the working-class carries with it the accumulation of skill handed down from one generation to another. This the capitalist looks upon as his property.

Summary.—Capitalistic production reproduces the separation between labour-power and the means of labour; reproduces the conditions necessary for the exploitation of the labourer; reproduces the capitalist relation.

CHAPTER XXIV.—CONVERSION OF SURPLUS-VALUE (s) INTO CAPITAL (C).

SECTION 1.—CAPITALIST PRODUCTION ON A PROGRESSIVELY INCREASING SCALE. TRANSITION OF THE LAWS OF PROPERTY THAT CHARACTERISE PRODUCTION OF COMMODITIES INTO LAWS OF CAPITALIST APPROPRIATION.

Accumulation of Capital.—The employment of surplus-value as capital is accumulation of capital.

Surplus-Product.—Only *mp* and means of subsistence can be turned into capital. Therefore part of the surplus-labour must have been spent in producing more means of production and subsistence than were required to replace the capital advanced. And these additional means will require additional labour.

Progressive Accumulation.—£10,000 C, say, begets Δ M or s of, say, £2,000. This £2,000 at the same rate begets £400. This £400, £20; etc. And all the time the original capital is still reproducing itself and producing s.

The Labourer.—The labourer, by the surplus-labour of one year, creates the *vc* that will employ additional labour the next year. The ownership of past unpaid labour is the one condition for the appropriation of present unpaid labour, and that on a constantly increasing scale.

Property.—Property becomes the right of the capitalist to appropriate the unpaid labour of the labourer, and to appropriate its product. The labourer cannot even appropriate his own product.

SECTION 2.—ERRONEOUS CONCEPTION BY POLITICAL ECONOMY OF REPRODUCTION ON A PROGRESSIVELY INCREASING SCALE.

Revenue.—Revenue, in the restricted sense, is the portion of the surplus-value that is not capitalised, that is expended in commodities to be consumed by the capitalist himself, or expended in labour that is bought for the satisfaction of the capitalist's own requirements.

Political Economy Right.—Political Economy is right in holding that the consumption of surplus-products by productive, as distinct from unproductive labour, is a feature of accumulation.

Political Economy Wrong.—But Political Economy

is wrong when it holds that all surplus-value that is changed into capital becomes *vc*. *s*, like C, is divided into *cc* (*mp*) and *vc* (labour-power).

SECTION 3.—SEPARATION OF *s* INTO C AND REVENUE. THE ABSTINENCE THEORY.

Revenue and Accumulation.—In Chapter XXIII. *s* was treated only as a fund for the individual consumption of the capitalist (revenue). In Chapter XXIV., thus far, *s* has been treated only as a fund for accumulation. Actually *s* is both.

Conflict.—At first, avarice is the ruling passion with the capitalist. Then lust of luxury comes in. Between these two, a conflict.

Malthus' Division of Labour.—"Accumulate, accumulate," is the word! Now as to classical economy, the labourer is only a machine for creating *s*, so to classical economy the capitalist is only a machine for accumulation. Therefore Malthus, about 1820, suggested that the industrial capitalist should do all the accumulating, and the other sharers in surplus-value (the landlords, etc.) should do all the spending.

Abstinence.—Senior was the first to substitute for capital as an instrument of production, the word "abstinence."

SECTION 4.—CIRCUMSTANCES THAT, INDEPENDENTLY OF THE PROPORTIONAL DIVISION OF SURPLUS-VALUE INTO CAPITAL AND REVENUE, DETERMINE THE AMOUNT OF ACCUMULATION. DEGREE OF EXPLOITATION OF LABOUR-POWER. PRODUCTIVITY OF LABOUR. GROWING DIFFERENCE IN AMOUNT BETWEEN CAPITAL EMPLOYED AND CAPITAL CONSUMED. MAGNITUDE OF CAPITAL ADVANCED.

Magnitude of s.—If the proportion in which *s* breaks up into revenue (see p. 133) and capital (to be re-employed in production) is given, the magnitude of the latter depends upon the absolute magnitude of *s*. Hence the circumstances that determine this last, determine the amount of accumulation.

1. Degree of Exploitation of Labour-Power.—The first of these circumstances is the degree of exploitation of labour-power. Thus far, in the investigation, it has been assumed that the wages paid are equal to the value of labour-power. Actually, however, there is often forcible reduction of wages below this value, and this transforms more or less of the labourer's necessary consumption fund into a fund for accumulation of capital.

Tendency of Capital.—The constant tendency of capital is to force the cost of labour down. From 1790 (about) to 1810, *e.g.*, the English farmers and landlords paid the agricultural labourers less than the minimum of wage in the form of wages, and made up the rest in parish relief.

Branches of Industry.—Marx then shows how, in every branch of industry, capital, having laid hold of the land and labour-power—the two primary creators of wealth—acquires a power of expansion that allows augmentation of accumulation beyond the limits apparently fixed by the magnitude of the capital itself, or by the value and mass of the *mp* employed. This is shown first in relation to industry generally. Additional labour can augment *s*, without a corresponding augmentation of *cc*. Then it is shown especially in relation to the extractive industries, agriculture, manufactures.

2. *Degree of p.*—As the productivity of labour increases, the mass of the surplus-product increases. Thus, the consumption of the capitalist (revenue) may increase without any falling off in the amount of accumulation. Or, if his consumption remains what it was, with the cheapening of commodities, part of what was revenue can go to accumulation. Further, with the increased *p* and the cheapening of commodities, the commodity—labour-power—cheapens, and the rate of *s* rises. The same *vc* now sets in motion more labour-power; the same *cc* is embodied in more *mp*. Accelerated accumulation even with the same C takes place.

Reaction on the Original Capital.—The development of *p* reacts on the original capital already functioning in the process of production. For the old instruments of labour are reproduced in a more productive form. And science gives capital a further power of expansion independently of the magnitude of *c*. So that the transmitted value of *cc* (see p. 49) increases with that increase of *p*.

Appearances and Realities.—Apparently this eternising of a constantly increasing capital-value is due to some intrinsic property of capital. Really, it is due to a property of labour-power, just as the real productive force of social labour (p. 70) is apparently an inherent property of capital, and as the apparent constant self-expansion of capital is really a constant appropriation of surplus-labour by the capitalist.

3. *Difference between Capital Employed and Consumed.*—As the accumulation of capital goes on, the difference between the capital employed and the capital actually consumed in a given time increases. Now, in the same proportion that the instruments of labour are wholly employed in forming products, but are only in part consumed, in that same proportion they are giving gratuitous service, like a natural force (steam, air, etc.), and are aiding accumulation.

4. *Magnitude of* C.—The magnitude of C deter-

mines the magnitude of *vc*, therefore the magnitude of labour-power employed, therefore the amount of *s* produced, therefore the amount of the value-increase to be divided into revenue and accumulated capital.

SECTION 5.—THE SO-CALLED LABOUR-FUND.

The Labour-Fund.—The economists have always loved to conceive social capital as a fixed magnitude. Especially Bentham and his followers hold that the total quantity of *vc* is a fixed magnitude, and this fabled magnitude they call the labour-fund.

Answers.—(1) The limits to the consumption on the part of the labourer laid down by the capitalistic system are only "natural" under that system; (2) the net product goes to the capitalist, and he divides it at will into revenue and accumulation-capital; (3) *vc*, and therefore the "labour-fund," is a variable fraction of social C, and that is a variable fraction of the social wealth, itself a variable quantity.

CHAPTER XXV.—THE GENERAL LAW OF CAPITALIST ACCUMULATION.

SECTION 1.—THE INCREASED DEMAND FOR LABOUR-POWER THAT ACCOMPANIES ACCUMULATION, THE COMPOSITION OF CAPITAL REMAINING THE SAME.

The Labourers.—In this chapter the influence of the growth of capital on the lot of the labouring class is considered. The most important factor is the composition of capital.

The Composition of Capital.—This may be looked at from the point of view of material (*mp* and labour-power).

Or it may be looked at from the point of view of value (*vc* and *cc*). And this gives its value-composition, and is the one now to be considered.

Total Social Capital.—The average composition of the many individual capitals in a particular branch of production gives the composition of the total capital in that branch.

The average of these averages in all branches of production gives the composition of the total social capital of a country. And this last is now considered.

Increase of the Proletariat.—Growth of C means also growth of *vc.* If, therefore, the composition of capital remains constant, the demand for labour and the subsistence fund of the labourers grow with the growth of C. Accumulation of C means increase of the proletariat.

Condition of the Proletariat.—Under the conditions of accumulation *thus far* considered, those most favourable to the labourer, the relation of dependence upon capital is endurable, and only becomes more extensive. Under these conditions, a larger portion of his surplus-product returns to the labourer as a means of payment. But nevertheless the exploitation remains.

Two Cases.—A rise in wages resulting from accumulation of C means one of two consequences.

1. That the rise in the price of labour continues because it does not interfere with the process of accumulation. In this case, an excess of capital makes the exploitable labour-power insufficient.

2. Or accumulation slackens in consequence of the rise in the price of labour, because the stimulus of gain is blunted. The primary cause of the slackening of accumulation, *i.e.* the disproportion between C and the labour-power exploitable, vanishes, and wages fall again. In this case a diminution of capital makes the exploitable labour-power in excess.

The Succession.—The absolute movements of the

accumulation of capital come first, and are followed by and reflected in the relative movements of the mass of exploitable labour-power.

Law.—The real law of capitalistic production that underlies the pretended "natural law of population," is, that the correlation between accumulation of C and rate of wages is the correlation between the unpaid labour turned into capital, and the additional paid labour necessary to work this new capital. A relation, indeed, between the unpaid and the paid labour of the same labouring population.

The System Still Maintained.—The very nature of the process of accumulation of capital excludes every diminution in the degree of exploitation, and every rise in wages that threatens the reproduction on a growing scale of the capitalistic relation.

SECTION 2.—RELATIVE DIMINUTION OF THE VARIABLE PART OF CAPITAL SIMULTANEOUSLY WITH THE PROGRESS OF ACCUMULATION AND OF THE CONCENTRATION THAT ACCOMPANIES IT.

p.—The general basis of the capitalistic system given, in the course of accumulation there comes a point at which the development of *p* becomes the most important factor in accumulation.

The degree of *p* is expressed in the relative extent of *mp* that one labourer, in a given time, with a given intensity of labour-power, (*l*), turns into products. It is expressed, therefore, in the diminution of the mass of labour in proportion to the mass of *mp* moved by it.

Consequence and Condition.—*mp* play two parts. The increase of some of them that follows upon increased *p*, is a consequence of the latter, *e.g.* raw material. The increase of others may be a consequence of increased *p*, but is also a necessary condition of the latter, *e.g.* machinery.

Technical and Value Composition.—This change in the technical composition of capital (p. 139) is reflected in the value or organic composition: *cc* increases and *vc* diminishes. A change reflected in its turn in the price of commodities. For in these, the relative magnitude of the element of price representing the value of *mp* or *cc* varies directly. The relative magnitude of the element of price that pays labour-power or *vc* varies inversely as the accumulation of capital.

Further Point.—Further, not only does the mass of the *mp* consumed by more productive labour increase. Their value, as compared with their mass, diminishes.

Relative and Absolute.—Although accumulation lessens the relative magnitude of *vc*, there may yet be a rise in the absolute magnitude, with a rise in the amount of C.

Primitive Accumulation.—On the basis of capitalistic production, co-operation can only take place on a large scale by increase of individual capitals, by *mp* and the means of subsistence becoming private property. A certain amount of accumulation of C in the hands of individuals is the necessary preliminary to capitalistic production (p. 39). And this is called primitive accumulation, and will be considered in the next chapter.

Converse.—Primitive accumulation is the necessary preliminary of capitalist production. Capitalist production, conversely, causes accelerated accumulation. And the mode of production and accumulation both cause the relative lessening of *vc*, as compared with *cc*.

Concentration.—At first, the number of individual capitalists grows. This is concentration of capital. It is limited by the amount of social wealth. And it leads to an antagonism in given spheres of production between the capitalists.

Centralisation.—Hence the expropriation of capitalist by capitalist, the swallowing up of the small capitalist by the large: centralisation of capital.

Laws.—The laws of centralisation of capital are to be developed later. In this place only three things are pointed out. (1) The battle of competition rages round the cheapening of commodities. This cheapness depends on *p*, and *p* depends on the scale of production. The large capitalist can produce on a larger scale than the small. (2) The minimum amount of individual C rises. (3) The credit system.

Converse.—With accumulation, centralisation grows. Conversely, centralisation helps accumulation.

Revolution in Production.—The capitalist method conquers branches of industry not yet under it; begets new ones; increases *p* in the old ones. And in all three ways the number of labourers falls in proportion to the *mp* they work upon.

SECTION 3.—PROGRESSIVE PRODUCTION OF A RELATIVE SURPLUS POPULATION OR INDUSTRIAL RESERVE ARMY.

Quantity and Quality.—Accumulation of capital is at first a quantitative extension. But a qualitative change follows, and *cc* increases at the expense of *vc*. And this at a greater rate than that of accumulation. Increasing accumulation and centralisation cause a more accelerated diminution of *vc* as compared with *cc*.

Surplus Population.—Hence capitalistic accumulation itself produces a surplus-labour population. In all spheres of production the decrease of *vc* is connected with production of surplus population. So that the labourer produces, along with accumulation of capital, the very means by which he becomes relatively surplus.

Converse.—And this surplus population, conversely,

becomes a new lever for accumulation. The movement of modern industry depends upon the transformation of part of the labouring population into a reserve army.

Increase of vc.—Even if *vc* absolutely (not relatively) increases, the number of labourers employed may fall, if the individual labourer yields more labour.

The Army and its Reserve.—The over-work of the army of employed condemns the reserve to an enforced idleness. The expansion and contraction of the reserve regulates wages. In stagnation and average times, the reserve weighs down the army; in over-production times, the reserve holds the pretensions of the army in check.

SECTION 4.—DIFFERENT FORMS OF THE RELATIVE SURPLUS POPULATION. THE GENERAL LAW OF CAPITALISTIC ACCUMULATION.

Forms.—The acute formation of a reserve army in crises; the chronic formation of a reserve army in dull times. And, apart from these, the floating, the latent, the stagnant forms.

Floating.—In the centres of modern industry the number of labourers employed falls, or if it increases absolutely, decreases relatively. Hence a floating surplus population.

In the automatic factories, boys can work until they

are grown up. Then they fall out and enter the ranks of the floating surplus population.

Latent.—The agricultural population constantly on the point of becoming the town proletariat.

Stagnant.—Those having irregular employment; maximum of working-time when it is forthcoming, and minimum wage.

Paupers.—The lowest sediment of the relative surplus population, exclusive of the "dangerous classes," makes up the paupers. Of these, there are three categories. (1) Those able to work, but having nothing to do. (2) Orphans and pauper children. (3) Those physically unable to work.

Law.—The general law of capitalistic accumulation is that the greater the social wealth, the greater the industrial reserve army.

More and more *mp* can be set in motion by less and less labour-power. Inverted form: the higher *p*, the more precarious is the condition of the labourer. As C accumulates, misery accumulates.

SECTION 5.—ILLUSTRATIONS OF THE GENERAL LAW OF CAPITALISTIC ACCUMULATION.

(*a*) England from 1846 to 1866.

Statistics.—This invaluable section is devoted to a series of statistics taken from Inland Revenue, Census, Blue-Book, and other Reports, all in proof of the general law given in the preceding paragraph. The statistics are so conclusive, and the law is of such moment, that the chief of them will be given in brief here without note or comment.

Relative Decrease of English Population shown by the steady decline of the yearly *absolute* increase.

1811-1821 . .	1·533 per cent.
1821-1831 . .	1·446 „
1831-1841 . .	1·326 „
1841-1851 . .	1·216 „
1851-1861 . .	1·141 „

Increase of Wealth.—Excess of yearly income of 1864 over 1853.

(1) Incomes—

Houses . .	3·5 per cent.	per year
Quarries . .	7·7 „	„
Mines . .	6·26 „	„
Iron-works .	3·63 „	„
Fisheries . .	5·21 „	„
Gas-works	11·45 „	„
Railways .	7·57 „	„

(2) Income tax—

1856 . .	Paid on £307,068,898.
1859 . .	„ 328,127,416.
1862 . .	„ 351,745,241.
1863 . .	„ 359,142,897.
1864 . .	„ 362,462,279.
1865 . .	„ 385,530,020.

(3) Coal—

1855	. 61,453,079 tons ;	worth	£16,113,167.
1864	. 92,787,873 „	„	23,197,968.

(4) Pig-iron—

1855	. 3,218,154 tons ;	worth	£8,045,385.
1864	. 4,767,951 „	„	11,919,877.

(5) Railroads—

1855	Length 8,054 mls.;	captl.,	£286,068,794.
1864	„ 12,789 „	„	425,719,613.

(6) Exports—

1846 . . .	£58,842,377.
1849 . . .	63,596,052.
1856 . . .	115,826,948.
1860 . . .	135,842,817.
1865 . . .	165,862,402.
1866 . . .	188,917,563.

Centralisation.—(1) 1851-1861, 5,016 smaller farms had been taken up into larger ones.

(2) 1815-1825, no personal estate over £1,000,000 came under the succession duty. 1825-1855 (30 years), 8 did. 1856-1859 (4 years), 4 did.

(3) Schedule D.

Gladstone and Fawcett.—Gladstone's Budget speeches of 1863 and 1864 are then quoted as evidence that "this intoxicating augmentation of wealth and power is entirely confined to classes of property.

Fawcett says, "the rich grow rapidly richer, whilst

there is no perceptible advance in the comfort enjoyed by the industrial classes."

Pauperism—

1855	. . 851,369	persons.	
1856	. . 877,767	"	
1863	. . 1,079,382	"	cotton famine years.
1864	. . 1,014,978	"	
1865	. . 971,433	"	

(*b*) The badly-paid strata of the British industrial class.

Carbon and Nitrogen.—Dr. Smith, charged by the Privy Council to investigate the conditions of the operatives in the cotton famine of 1862, calculated that, to avert starvation diseases, the weekly food of adult men and women should contain 28,600 grains of carbon, and 1,330 grains of nitrogen. The actual consumption of the miserable operatives was found to be, in December 1862, 29,211 grains of carbon and 1,295 grains of nitrogen weekly.

In 1863, seven classes of operatives were examined. In one only of the indoor workers was the average supply of nitrogen just over the starvation disease-level; in another, just under; in others, deficiency of nitrogen and carbon.

Agricultural Labourers.—The agricultural labours ers examined in the same way gave as results :—more than one-fifth of them with too little carbon food; more than one-third with too little nitrogen food. In Berkshire, Oxford, Somersetshire, insufficiency of nitrogen food, the average diet.

Housing of the Poor.—The greater the centralisation of the means of production, the greater the crowding of the labourers, the worse their dwellings, the higher relatively their rent. In 1801, there were only five towns in England with more than 50,000 inhabitants. In 1867, there were twenty-eight. Hence, between 1847 and 1864, the frightened middle-class pass, for self-preservation, ten sanitary acts. London, Newcastle-on-Tyne, Bradford, Bristol is the succession from worse to bad.

(*c*) The nomad population.

Nomads.—Originally agricultural, now in great part industrial, working at lime-burning, railway-making, etc., the light infantry of capital, hurled by it now on this point, now on that. A flying column of pestilence, either camping or vegetating in hut-barracks built by the railway contractor, and charged for at the rate of from one shilling to four shillings a week.

Coal Miners.—Marx then gives a description of the terrible house conditions of the miners. For these fearful details the reader is referred to pp. 683-685 of "Capital."

(*d*) Effects of crisis on the best paid part of the working-class.

Crisis of 1866.—From pp. 686-689, quotations are given from the London newspapers of 1866 to show the awful condition of things among even the skilled mechanics at the east-end of London after the failures of Overend, Gurney, and others, and after the crisis in the iron ship-building trade.

Belgium.—As Belgium is often quoted as the paradise of "free labour," Marx gives the following comparative figures.

Normal Belgian working-family yearly wage . .	1,068	francs.
A prisoner's food costs yearly	1,112	„
A soldier's „ „ .	1,473	„
A sailor's „ „ .	1,828	„

(*e*) The British agricultural proletariat.

The Law Again.—As English agriculture progresses, the English agricultural labourer retrogresses.

1740-1808.—Modern agriculture in England dates from about 1740. Between 1737 and 1747 wages fell 25 per cent. In 1771 the agricultural labourer was worse off than in the fourteenth century. Yet, in 1771, he was better off than he has ever been since. Thus, his average wage, expressed in pints of wheat, was, in 1771, 90 pints; in 1797, 65; in 1808, 60.

1795 and 1814.—In Northamptonshire, in 1795, the total income of a family of six was £29 18s.; the deficit made good by the parish (p. 136), £6 14s. 5d

In 1814 the total income of a family of five was £36 2s.; the deficit made good by the parish, £18 6s. 4d. Nominal wage had risen; real wage fallen.

Corn-Law Agitation. — The bourgeois and the landed proprietors were at this time by the ears. The former exposed the conditions of the agricultural labourer; the latter exposed the conditions of the factory operatives.

Repeal.—The repeal of the Corn-Laws gave a great stimulus to agricultural industry. Improved drainage, stall-feeding, manuring, treatment of soils, use of steam, etc.

Centralisation.—In 1851-1871, farms under 20 acres fell in number 900; farms from 50-75 acres fell 1,883; farms under 100 acres all fell. But farms from 300-500 acres rose 639; farms from 500-1,000 rose 1,159; farms over 1,000 rose 90.

Area and Labourers.—Area under cultivation increased, between 1846 and 1856, by 464,119 acres.

Number of labourers between 1851 and 1861 fell 78,179.

Conclusion.—So that, with extension and intension of culture, accumulation of capital incorporated in the soil, increase of products, of rents, of profits, there was depopulation.

Criminals.—According to the Report of the Commissioners on Transportation and Penal Servitude, prisoners are better nourished than, and only do half as much work as, the agricultural labourer.

Table.—Weekly nutriment in ounces.

Working coachmaker .	190·82
Sailor	187·06
Convict	183·69
Soldier	143·98
Compositor	125·16
Agricultural labourer . .	139·08

Dwellings.—Pp. 701-718 are taken up with facts and figures showing the miserable and terrible conditions of the dwellings of the agricultural labourer. Here only one or two general points can be noted, but the reader is urged to look through these pages of "Capital" for stimulus and inspiration.

There is no law compelling the farmer to build labourers' dwellings.

Between 1851 and 1861, the agricultural population grew $5\frac{1}{3}$ per cent.; the houseroom for them fell $4\frac{1}{2}$ per cent.

The labourer often has to walk six or eight miles to his work.

The close villages owned by one or two larger landlords give rise to the open villages owned by many small landlords, and the haunt of the building speculator.

The Nuisances Removal Acts are administered by the very proprietors of these dens.

An Example.—5,375 cottages of agricultural labourers were visited by Dr. Hunter. 2,195 of them had only one bedroom; 2,930 only two bedrooms; 254 more than two.

Countries. — Special details are given of places in Bedfordshire, Berkshire, Buckinghamshire, Cambridgeshire, Essex, Herefordshire, Huntingdonshire, Lincolnshire, Kent, Northamptonshire, Wiltshire, Worcestershire.

Relative and Surplus Population.—Emigration to towns, centralisation of farms, turning of arable into pasture-land, introduction of machinery, formation of relative surplus population, all go hand in hand. And yet the land, in spite of its relative surplus population, is under-manned. This is seen locally where the efflux of men into the towns is most marked and, *e.g.*, temporarily at harvest time. There are always too many agricultural labourers for the ordinary—too few for the extraordinary—needs of the cultivation of the soil.

Gang System.—This temporary or local deficiency of labour leads to the employment of women and children, and such amenities as the gang system of the eastern counties. The gang consists of from 10 to 50 women, young persons (generally females only), children of both sexes, headed by the gang-master. He is the recruiting sergeant, is paid contract piece-work wage by the farmer, and exploits his gang. From six to eight months in the year the gang marches five to seven miles daily, is overworked, and morally ruined. The arrangement exists for the benefit of the large farmer and the landlord.

(*f*) Ireland.

Population—

1841	8,222,664.
1851	6,623,985.
1861	5,850,309.
1866	5,500,000 (about)

Emigration—

1851-1865 (14 years), .	1,591,487.
1861-1865 (4 of the 14), .	500,000 (about)

Houses.—The number of inhabited houses fell from 1851-1861 by 52,990.

Centralisation.—In the same ten years, the holdings of 15 to 30 acres increased 61,000; those of over 30 acres increased 109,000; whilst the total number of farms fell 120,000.

Tables.—Five tables are then given, which prove, in respect to Ireland, the general law of capitalistic accumulation. They are,—(A) live stock; (B) cultivated land, 1861-1865; (C) a similar table, much more in detail, for 1864 and 1865; (D) income tax returns (a steady rise, with one very slight fall in 1864); (E) income from profits in 1864 and 1865.

Surplus-Produce.—Centralisation and the turning

of arable into pasture-land mean a larger quantity, relatively, of surplus-produce. The total produce decreased, but the surplus-produce fraction of it actually increased in Ireland from 1860 to 1865. And the money-value of it also rose.

Emigration.—The amount of emigration has been enormous. And yet the relative surplus population remains as large as ever; wages do not rise; oppression and misery do not lessen. The advance of agriculture has atoned for the emigration.

Linen Manufacture.—The one great industry of Ireland (linen manufacture) employs few adult men and only a few people altogether. It produces a relative surplus population within its own sphere. It begets domestic industries (p. 97).

Wages.—There has been an apparent rise, from 1849 to 1869, of 50 to 60 per cent. But a real fall, as the price of the means of subsistence has more than doubled in the time.

England and Ireland.—England is an industrial country, and the industrial army recruits itself from the country districts. Ireland is an agricultural country, and the agricultural reserve army recruits itself from the towns, to which the expelled agricultural labourers have fled.

PART VIII.—THE SO-CALLED PRIMITIVE ACCUMULATION.

CHAPTER XXVI.—The Secret of Primitive Accumulation.

The Circle To-day.—Money becomes capital. Capital begets surplus-value. Surplus-value begets capital. Tracing it backwards, accumulation of capital presupposes surplus-value; surplus-value presupposes capitalistic production; capitalistic production presupposes primitive accumulation (the previous accumulation of Adam Smith).

The Economists.—The political economists preach the pretty fable of the one class diligent and the other class lazy; the reward of the one in having capital, of the other in having nothing. With them everything is idyllic.

The Truth.—The truth is that historically everything is conquest, brutality, robbery—in a word, force. Primitive accumulation is the separation by force of the producer from the means of production.

Evolution of the Wage-Labourer.—The economic structure of capitalistic society has grown out of the economic structure of feudal society. The labourer, to be "free," had (1) to cease to be attached to the soil, to cease to be a serf; (2) he had to cease to be under the rule of the guilds; (3) he had to be robbed of the means of production.

The Capitalist.—The industrial capitalist, on his part, had (1) to fight the feudal lord; (2) to fight the guilds; (3) to rob the labourer of the means of production.

Date.—The transformation of feudal exploitation into capitalistic exploitation begins, here and there, in certain of the Mediterranean towns, as early as the fourteenth or fifteenth century. Formally, the capitalistic era dates from the sixteenth century.

Basis.—The basis of the whole process of primitive accumulation is the expropriation of the agricultural labourer from that means of production upon which he works—viz. the soil.

CHAPTER XXVII.—EXPROPRIATION OF THE AGRICULTURAL POPULATION FROM THE LAND.

Fourteenth and Fifteenth Centuries.—By the end of the fourteenth century, serfdom had vanished. The mass of the population were free peasant-proprietors. What wage-labourers there were consisted of peasants working in their leisure time on the large estates, and a very few actual wage-labourers, who, none the less, owned four acres of land at least and a cottage, whilst they, like all the rest, owned the common lands, feeding cattle on them, taking wood, turf, etc., from them.

The Prelude.—The prelude to the revolution that laid the foundation of the capitalist mode of production covers 1460-1510. The breaking up of the bands of feudal retainers gave rise to the first proletariat. The feudal lords drove the peasants from the land and stole the common lands. Arable land was turned into pasture.

1489.—Legislation set in against this revolution. An Act of Henry VII., 1489, forbade the destruction of all "houses of husbandry" with twenty acres of land attached. This was renewed by an Act, 1534, in Henry VIII's. time.

1533.—The Act of 1533 states that some owners have 24,000 sheep, and limits the number to 2,000. But all the legislation and the cry of the people during 150 years against the expropriation of the small farmers and the peasants was of no avail.

The Four Acres.—Efforts were made to retain the four acres of land around the cottage of the agricultural wage-labourer. Thus, in 1627, Roger Crocker of Front Mill was condemned for having built upon his manor a cottage minus the four acres of land. In 1638, a Royal Commission was appointed to enforce the old laws, and especially the four acres one. And, in the time of Cromwell, the building of a house within four miles of London, minus the four acres, was forbidden.

The Reformation.—Economically, the Reformation was spoliation of the property of the Church, the driving out of hereditary sub-tenants, the centralising of their holdings, the confiscation of the guaranteed property of the poor in the tithes of the Church.

Poor-Rate.—In the year 1601, the forty-third of the reign of Elizabeth, the first poor-rate was introduced. In the year 1641, the sixteenth of the reign of Charles I, this poor-rate was declared perpetual, and held until, in the year 1834, it was replaced by a harsher law.

Yeomanry.—In 1690-1700, the independent peasants or yeomanry were more in number than the farmers. By 1780 they had vanished, and by 1800 the last trace of the common land of the agricultural labourer was gone.

The Restoration.—Economically, the Restoration was the carrying, by legal means, of abolition of the feudal tenure of land; indemnification of the State by taxes levied on the labourers; vindication of the rights of modern private property in estates that had only been held under feudal tenure.

The Revolution.—Economically, the Revolution was theft of State lands without any legal ceremony The spoliation of the Church, and this theft of State lands, founded the English oligarchy of to-day. The capitalists helped, as they wanted (1) free trade in land; (2) the extension of modern agriculture; (3) more "free" agricultural labourers.

Advance of Civilisation.—The forcible theft of communal lands, with the turning of arable to pasture, began at the end of the fifteenth and ran into the sixteenth century. And legislation opposed it. But in the seventeenth the law itself did the thieving from the people. The parliamentary form of this particular theft is Acts for the enclosure of commons.

1801-1831.—Between the years 1801 and 1831, 3,511,770 acres of common land were stolen from the people by the landlords, without any compensation.

Clearing of Estates.—The final process of expropriating the agricultural labourer from the soil is the clearing of estates, seen at its worst in the Highlands. The chiefs of the clans (the Argyles and the Sutherlands) transformed their nominal rights into rights of private property, and drove their clansmen out by main force. The Gaels were even forbidden, in the eighteenth century, to emigrate. Thus, they were forced into the ranks of the industrial population of the towns.

The Duchess of Sutherland.—A typical example is the Duchess of Sutherland. Between 1814 and 1820 this woman drove out, literally by fire and sword, 15,000 of her clan, and stole 794,000 acres of land to make a sheep-walk. The stolen land she divided into twenty-nine sheep-farms, looked after by twenty-nine families, mostly English. Later, the sheep-walks were replaced by deer-preserves. At first, she "allowed" her clansmen 6,000 waste acres on the seashore that had thus far brought in no income. Rent, 2s. 6d. per acre. But, as her clansmen began to catch fish, she let the seashore to the Billingsgate fishmongers, and "cleared" her estates finally.

Summary.—The spoliation of the Church property under the Reformation, the abolition of feudal tenure under the Restoration, the theft of State lands under the Revolution, the theft of the common lands, the clearing of estates, are the chief phases in primitive accumulation.

CHAPTER XXVIII.—Bloody Legislation Against the Expropriated, from the End of the Fifteenth Century. Forcing Down of Wages by Acts of Parliament.

Vagabonds.—The "free" proletariat could not be absorbed by the nascent manufacture as rapidly as it was set free. Nor could it at once and easily change its old habits. Hence, at the end of the fifteenth and through the sixteenth century, vagabonds and laws against vagabonds.

Laws.—Marx then gives the details of the infamous laws, with their whippings and imprisonments and brandings and iron-rings and hangings, in England and abroad (pp. 758-761). Nowadays these laws are not needed, because a working-class has been evolved that, by education, tradition, habit, looks upon the present conditions of production as "laws of nature."

Wage-Labour Legislation.—He then gives an epitome of the laws from 1349-1813, regulating the maximum of wage, but never the minimum. In 1794 an attempt was made to legalise the minimum rate, but it failed. In 1813 the laws for regulation of wage were repealed. They were not wanted, as the capitalist could regulate them by his private legislation in his own factory.

Contract.—In the breaking of contracts only civil action can be brought against the master, but criminal action against the man.

Trade Unions.—The barbarous laws against Trade Unions fell in part in 1825, in part again in 1859, and on June 29, 1871, Trade Unions were legally recognised.

CHAPTER XXIX.—Genesis of the Capitalist Farmer.

Stages.—(1) The bailiff, himself a serf; (2) the farmer, provided by the landlord with seed, cattle, and tools, exploiting some wage-labour; (3) the half farmer, who advances part of the stock-in-trade, the landlord advancing the other, the total product divided between them in pre-fixed proportion; (4) the farmer proper, making his capital breed by employing wage labour, and paying part of the surplus-product as rent.

Common Lands.—The usurpation of the common lands enabled him to augment his stock, and yielded him more manure.

Fall in Value of Gold.—The fall in the value of the precious metals in the sixteenth century lowered wages. The price of corn, etc., rose; rents (calculated on the old value of money) fell.

Middlemen.—The lion's share always falls to the middleman. Examples—financiers, merchants, shopkeepers, lawyers, M.P.'s, priests.

CHAPTER XXX.—REACTION OF THE AGRICULTURAL REVOLUTION ON INDUSTRY. CREATION OF THE HOME MARKET FOR INDUSTRIAL CAPITAL.

Means of Subsistence and mp.—When a part of the agricultural population is set "free," their means of subsistence are also set free, and become *vc.* So also the raw materials, dependent upon home agriculture, are set free, and become *cc.* 2*b* (p. 41) and 2 are no longer means of independent existence for labour, but a means of commanding it.

Home Market.—Further, this expropriation of the agricultural labourer not only sets free, and at the disposal of the industrial capitalist, the labourers, their means of subsistence, and the raw material they used, but it creates the home market. The means of subsistence and the raw material they used have now become commodities.

Separation between Agriculture and Manufacture.—With the expropriation and the separation of the expropriated from *mp,* rural domestic industry is destroyed, and the process of separation between agriculture and manufacture sets in. This is not complete under manufacture, as the men and industries got rid of in one form turn up again in lessened numbers and worse conditions in another. England, *e.g.*, is at one time a corn cultivator, at another a cattle breeder, and thus the extent of peasant cultivation varies. But modern industry replaced handicrafts and domestic industries by machinery, and the lasting basis of capitalistic agriculture completes the separation.

CHAPTER XXXI.—Genesis of the Industrial Capitalist.

Mediæval Capital.—The middle ages handed down two distinct forms of capital—usurer's and merchant's. These were hindered from turning into industrial capital, in the country, by the feudal system; in the town, by the guilds. These hindrances vanish with the vanishing of the feudal system.

Momenta of Primitive Accumulation.—The essence of primitive accumulation is the separation of the labourer from *mp* and from the product he produces. To this process, momentum was given by the discovery of gold and silver in America, the extirpation or enslavement of the American aborigines, the looting of East India, the slave trade of Africa, the European commercial wars.

Countries.—Spain, Portugal, Holland, France, England, were the chief primitive accumulation lands. In England, by 1800, there was a systematic combination, including the colonial system, dependent on brute force; the national debt, taxation, protection, dependent on State force.

East India Company.—The monopolies of this

Company led to primitive accumulation on a giant scale, often without the advance of a shilling.

Colonies.—The treatment and exploitation of the aborigines were worst in plantation colonies, such as the West Indies, intended for export trade only, and in rich countries, such as India, given over to plunder. But the Puritans, *e.g.*, were not far behind in the good work, even in the colonies proper.

Holland.—Holland, the first country to develop the colonial system, was, in 1640, at its greatest height of commercial greatness. And in 1648, its people were more overworked and oppressed and poorer than those of the rest of Europe.

National Debt.—The system of public credit, *i.e.* of national debts, originating in Venice and Genoa in the middle ages, became general under manufacture. The colonial system forced it on, and it first took root in Holland. It is one of the most powerful levers of primitive accumulation, as investment of money under this system involves no trouble and no risk.

International Credit.—Venice, in her decay, lends to Holland the materials for her primitive accumulation. Holland, in turn, to England, and England to the United States.

Taxation.—The modern system of taxation was the necessary complement to a national debt, the interest of which must be met out of the public revenue. Over-taxation helps in the forcible expropriation of the lower middle-class. Indeed, the part played in this expropriation by the national debt and the fiscal system of to-day has misled Cobbett and others to see in this the primary and not the secondary cause of misery.

Protection.—The system of protection was an artificial means of manufacturing manufacturers, of expropriating individual labourers, of capitalising the national means of production and subsistence, of hurrying on the transition from the mediæval to the capitalist method of production.

Liverpool.—Liverpool's method of primitive accumulation was the slave trade. In 1730 she employed, in this trade, 15 ships; in 1751, 53; in 1760, 74; in 1770, 96; in 1792, 132.

CHAPTER XXXII.—HISTORICAL TENDENCY OF CAPITALISTIC ACCUMULATION.

The Future.—This chapter will be to many, especially to the hopeful, of the highest interest. The same inexorable logic and the same scientific calm with which the analysis of value, of labour-power, of capital, of accumulation, has been conducted, are here brought to bear upon the question of the next stage in economic evolution. And this is not a question of what we hope may be; it is a question of what history says must be.

Private Property.—Private property, based upon the labour of its owner, self-earned private property, has been replaced by capitalistic private property, based on the labour of others than the owner of the property. And this will give way to individual property based on the acquisitions of the capitalist era, based on co-operation and the possession in common of the land and of *mp.*

Petty Industry.—The first form of private property implied the private property of the labourer in his means of production; and this is the foundation of all small industry, agricultural, manufacturing, or both. This form excludes the concentration of *mp*, co-operation, division of labour within each separate process of production, the productive application of natural forces by society, and the free development of the productive powers of society. At a certain stage of its development this petty industry brings forth the material agencies for its own destruction.

Capitalistic.—Under petty industry, the labourer working for himself was expropriated. Under modern industry, the capitalist exploiting others will be expropriated.

Causes.—The causes of this inevitable result are immanent in capitalistic production. (1) Centralisation of capital in few hands; (2) socialisation of labour; (3) internationalisation of capital; (4) increase of misery; (5) class consciousness of the workers; (6) their revolt.

Differences.—The earlier transformation of scattered private property, arising from individual labour, into capitalistic private property, was a very protracted, violent, difficult expropriation of the many by the few.

The coming transformation of capitalistic private property, based on socialised production, into socialised property, will be the less protracted, less violent, less difficult expropriation of the few by the many.

CHAPTER XXXIII.—THE MODERN THEORY OF COLONISATION.

Colonies.—In Western Europe, we have a ready-made world of capital. In the colonies, the capitalist *régime* comes into collision with the resistance of the producer, who prefers employing his labour-power for himself. Hence, in the colonies, the political economist proclaims that which he denies in Europe, viz. :—that capitalistic production is impossible without expropriation of the labourer.

Wakefield's Discoveries.—Mr. E. G. Wakefield, in his "England and America," 1833, discovers (1) that as long as the labourer can accumulate for himself (*i.e.* as long as he owns *mp*), capitalistic accumulation and production are impossible; (2) that in free colonies, where the bulk of the soil is public property, expropriation of the labourer from the soil cannot occur, and capitalistic accumulation and production are impossible; (3) that not only is no surplus-labour population produced, but the wage-labourer himself is not reproduced, as he is constantly transformed into an independent producer; (4) that the degree of exploitation is very low, and the labourer is very independent;

(5) that the supply of wage-labour is neither constant, regular, nor sufficient; (6) that there is a "barbarising tendency of dispersion" of producers and products.

His Scheme.—His "systematic colonisation" scheme was to put by Government an artificial price upon the virgin soil, so that the immigrant *must* work a long time as a wage-labourer; the fund thus raised to be used to import new wage-labourers to take the place of any fortunate enough to save the value of the prohibitory price of a piece of land.

Results.—The result of this plan, enforced by Act of Parliament, was the turning of the stream of emigration away from the English colonies to the United States. But the scheme was soon superfluous. In America, Australia, everywhere, the centralisation of capital, national debts, taxes, speculation, exploitation are in full swing, and the "reserve army" has formed.

The import of this glance at the colonies is that there the political economist discovers the law he cannot see at work here—that the capitalist mode of production and accumulation, and, therefore, capitalist private property, are based upon the annihilation of self-earned private property, upon the expropriation of the labourer.

Works quoted.—The list of books, reports, journals, quoted from by Marx in "Capital," is 352 in number.

THE END.

Made in the USA
Monee, IL
04 November 2026

67385026R00105